To Nancy S. T., Philip, T. L., and Christina K. L.

IELTS™

Rhyming Memory
Dictionary

Richard Lee, Ph.D.

COLUMBIA PRESS

Copyright © 2012 Richard Lee, Columbia Press

All rights reserved.

No part of this book may be reproduced or distributed in any form or by any means without the written permission of the copyright owner.

All inquiries should be addressed to:

Columbia Press

803-470 Granville Street

Vancouver, BC V6C 1V5

ISBN-13: 978-0-9879778-2-3

INTRODUCTION

Columbia IELTS Rhyming Memory Dictionary is compiled to help you memorize 800 most tested real IELTS key words fast to raise your score!

Here are the outstanding features of this dictionary:

- 800 most tested real IELTS key words with pronunciation guides, definitions, rhyming IELTS words, grammar tips, and synonyms;
- Each key entry has a sample sentence in the form of a Sentence Completion question with answer key to test your readiness for the IELTS;
- Easy rhyming memory techniques to help you master hundreds of most difficult IELTS words to score higher guaranteed!

Columbia IELTS Rhyming Memory Dictionary is your word Bible! With our proven memory techniques, never will you have to worry about memorizing IELTS words; for they will rhyme all their way into your ears like music: memorizing words is this simple, easy, and fun!

A

ab.di.cate [ˈæbdɪˌkeɪt] *v.* to yield; to give up

rhyming memory sound – ate

ab.ro.gate *v.* to abolish; to repeal

ca.lum.ni.ate *v.* to accuse falsely

Grammar Tips: -cating, -cated, -cates

Synonym: abandon

Sentence Completion: choose one rhyming word above to complete the sentence.

The official was forced to _____ his position and was sent to prison for life.

Answer: *abdicate*

a.be.yance [əˈbeɪəns] *n.* a temporary postponement

rhyming memory sound – ance

nui.sance *n.* harm; injury

an.no.yance *n.* the act of annoying

Grammar Tips: -abeyant *adj.*

Synonym: doldrums

Sentence Completion: choose one rhyming word above to complete the sentence.

The judge held the question in_____until he had the information necessary to make a decision.

Answer: *abeyance*

ab.jure [æbˈdʒʊr] *v.* to renounce upon oath; to repudiate

rhyming memory sound – ure

con.jure v to evoke a spirit; to cast a spell

en.dure *v.* to carry on despite hardships

Grammar Tips: –jured, -juring, -ures; -abjuration *n.*,

-abjurer *n.*

Synonym: renounce

Sentence Completion: choose one rhyming word above to complete the sentence.

Some of the Roman Emperors tried to make Christians_____ their religion.

Answer: *abjure*

ab.ro.gate [ˈæbrəˌgeɪt] *v.* to abolish; to repeal

rhyming memory sound –ate

em.u.late *v.* to strive to equal or excel; to imitate

fa.bri.cate *v.* to construct; to invent

Grammar Tips: -gated, -gating, -gates; -abrogation *n.*

Synonym: nullify

Sentence Completion: choose one rhyming word above to complete the sentence.

No one can_____ our right to freedom of speech.

Answer: *abrogate*

ac.cen.tu.ate [æk'sentʃuˌeɪt] *v.* to give force to; draw attention to   ***rhyming memory sound –ate***

ac.ce.le.rate *v.* to cause to move faster

ac.cu.mu.late ..*v*...to gather or pile up little by little

Grammar Tips: -tuated, -tuating, -tuates, -accentuation *n.*

Synonym: emphasize

Sentence Completion: choose one rhyming word above to complete the sentence.

President Barack Obama, once a stern critic of the war, did his best to_____the positive in a speech to US troops last week.

Answer: *accentuate*

a.cer.bic [ə'sɜrbɪk] *adj.* sharp or bitter in smell or taste
rhyming memory sound –ic

rus.tic   *adj.* rural; pastoral; bucolic

bom.bas.tic   *adj.* high-sounding but meaningless; ostensibly lofty in style

Grammar Tips: -acerbity *n.*

Synonym: biting

Sentence Completion: choose one rhyming word above to complete the sentence.

A lot of Hollywood films tend to be bloated, _____, and loud.

Answer: *bombastic*

a.cri.mo.nious [ˌækrɪˈmoʊniəs]   *adj.* bitter; hostile

rhyming memory sound –onious

par.si.mo.nious *adj.*   stingy; frugal; mean

sanc.ti.mo.nious *adj.* hypocritically devout; self-righteous

Grammar Tips: -acrimoniously *adv.*, -acrimoniousness *n.*

-acromony *n.*

Synonym: bitter

Sentence Completion: choose one rhyming word above to complete the sentence.

Jennifer went through a terribly_____ divorce.

Answer: *acrimonious*

a.cu.men [ˈækjəmən] *n.* mental keenness; shrewdness
rhyming memory sound –umen

al.bu.men *n.* the white of an egg

ce.ru.men *n.* earwax

Grammar Tips: Latin origin: *acuere*.

Synonym: *astuteness*

Sentence Completion: choose one rhyming word above to complete the sentence.

Shakespeare's business_____made him a fortune by writing plays.

Answer: *acumen*

aes.the.tic [esˈθetɪk] *adj.* pertaining to beauty or art

rhyming memory sound -etic

as.ce.tic *adj.* self-denying; abstinent; austere

her.me.tic *adj.* deliberately staying separate from other people

Grammar Tips: -aesthetics *pl.*,-aesthetic *n.*

Synonym: beautiful

Sentence Completion: choose one rhyming word above to complete the sentence.

Perfect teeth - white, straight and evenly aligned - may be the ideal in America, but that _____ is not for everyone.

Answer: *aesthetic*

al.lu.sion [əˈluʒ(ə)n] *n.* a statement that refers to something in an indirect way   ***rhyming memory sound –usion***

de.lu.sion *n.* the act of deluding

il.lu.sion *n.* the state of being intellectually deceived or led astray

Grammar Tips: -allusive *adj.*, -allusively *adv.*,

-allusiveness *n.*

Synonym: insinuation

Sentence Completion: choose one rhyming word above to complete the sentence.

A burning blush upon the girl's face showed that she understood the old man's _____.

Answer: *allusion*

am.bi.guous [æmˈbɪgjuəs] *adj.*. unclear   *rhyming memory sound –iguous*

con.ti.guous *adj.* next to each othere or joining each other

e.xi.guous *adj.* extremely small in quantity

Grammar Tips: -ambiguously *adj.*, -ambiguousness *n.*

Synonym: obscure

Sentence Completion: choose one rhyming word above to complete the sentence.

But after he made a marginally_____statement about taxes, Mr Norquist jumped on the phone.

Answer: *ambiguous*

a.nec.dote [ˈænəkˌdoʊt] *n.* short and funny account of an event   *rhyming memory sound –ote*

an.ti.dote *n.* a remedy to counteract the effects of poison

lo.co.mote *v.* to move about

Grammar Tips: -anecdotes or -anecdota *pl.*, -anecdalist *n.*

Synonym: story

Sentence Completion: choose one rhyming word above to complete the sentence.

My professors would be more eloquent in a theoretical rebuttal of that charge, but I want to counter it myself with a personal _____.

Answer: *anecdote*

an.ti.pa.thy [ænˈtɪpəθi] *n.* intense dislike   *rhyming memory sound –athy*

wra.thy *n.* angry; wrathful

em.pa.thy *n.* identification with the feelings of others

Grammar Tips: -antipathize *v.*

Synonym: animosity

Sentence Completion: choose one rhyming word above to complete the sentence.

There has always been _____ between the two rival companies.

Answer: *antipathy*

app.ro.ba.tion [ˌæproʊˈbeɪʃ(ə)n] *n.* praise; approval
rhyming memory sound –ation

e.mi.gra.tion *n.* leaving one country to live in another

ex.al.ta.tion *n.* glory or honor

Grammar Tips: -approbatory *adj.*

Synonym: approval

Sentence Completion: choose one rhyming word above to complete the sentence.

The cheering crowd welcomed the Hollywood star with _____ and admiration..

Answer: *approbation*

as.ce.tic. [əˈsetɪk] *adj.* self-denying, abstinent, auster

rhyming memory sound –etic

ki.ne.tic *adj.* relating to motion, characterized by movement

pa.the.tic *adj.* arousing scornful pity

Grammar Tips: -ascetic *n.*, -ascetically *adv.*, -asceticism *n.*

Synonym: abstemious

Sentence Completion: choose one rhyming word above to complete the sentence.

In order to be healthy and slim, the beautiful actress keeps an_____ diet of rice and beans.

Answer: *ascetic*

as.per.sion [əˈspɝʒən] *n.* a curse, expression of ill-will
rhyming memory sound –ersion

a.ver.sion *n.* a feeling of repugnance toward something

d.iver.sion *n.* the act of diverting from doing something

Grammar Tips: -aspersions *n.*

Synonym: slander

Sentence Completion: choose one rhyming word above to complete the sentence.

As far as I am concerned, I don't mean to cast any _____ on people smoking outside.

Answer: *aspersion*

as.si.duous [əˈsɪdʒuəs] *n.* diligent; persistent

rhyming memory sound –uous

con.spi.cuous *adj.* obvious to the eye or mind

in.con.gruous *adj.* not harmonious

Grammar Tips: -assiduously *adv.*, -assiduousness *n.*, -assiduity *n.*

Synonym: sedulous

Sentence Completion: choose one rhyming word above to complete the sentence.

They have finally finished the construction of the city's tallest building after two years of _____ labor.

Answer: *assiduous*

B

baffle [ˈbæf(ə)l] *v.* to confuse; to bewilder   *rhyming memory sound –affle*

raffle *n.* a competition in which you win a prize if the number on your ticket is the same as the number on the prize

snaffle *n.* a bit for a horse that is jointed in the middle and has rings on either end where the reins are attached

Grammar Tips: -baffled, -baffling, -baffles; -bafflement *n.*
-baffler *n.*, -bafflingly *adv.*

Synonym: frustrate

Sentence Completion: choose one rhyming word above to complete the sentence.

Women_____him, he never seems to gain a clear understanding of them.

Answer: *baffle*

blan.dish.ment ['blændiʃmənt] *n.* flattery; allurement

rhyming memory sound –ent

dis.sent *v.* to withhold assent; to differ in opinion

cir.cum.vent *v.* to go around; to avoid

Grammar Tips: -blandish *v.*

Synonym: allurement

Sentence Completion: choose one rhyming word above to complete the sentence.

Jennifer was able to_____the school's regulations by taking more AP courses for credits.

Answer: *circumvent*

boon [bun] *n.* a benefit; a blessing; a favor

rhyming memory sound –oon

lam.poon *v.* to ridicule with satire

ty.coon *n.* a wealthy powerful businessman or industrialist

Grammar Tips: -boon *adj.*

                                             Synonym: advantage

Sentence Completion: choose one rhyming word above to complete the sentence.

The good weather has been a_____for many farmers this year.

                                              Answer: *boon*

brusque [brʊsk] *adj.* abrupt in manner; blunt; rough

rhyming memory sound –usque/usk

cusk *n.* a large edible North Atlantic fish of the cod family

tusk *n.* an elongated, pointed tooth (as of an elephant or walrus)

Grammar Tips: -brusquely *adv.*, -brusqueness *n.*

                                             Synonym: abrupt

Sentence Completion: choose one rhyming word above to complete the sentence.

The bus driver's_____manner offended a lot of tourists in the city.

Answer: *brusque*

bur.geon [ˈbɜrdʒən] v. to flourish; to grow rapidly

rhyming memory sound –urgeon

stur.geon *n.* a large fish that lives in northern oceans, rivers, and lakes, and whose roe is made into caviar

sur.geon *n.* a doctor or specialist who practices surgery

Grammar Tips: –geoned, -geoning, -geons

Synonym: accelerate

Sentence Completion: choose one rhyming word above to complete the sentence.

Seeds begin to_____at the beginning of spring.

Answer: *burgeon*

bur.nish [ˈbɜrnɪʃ] v. to polish; to shine *rhyming memory sound –urnish*

fur.nish v. to provide with; to supply

re.fu.rnish v. to give again

Grammar Tips: -burnished, burnishing, burnishes

Synonym: polish

Sentence Completion: choose one rhyming word above to complete the sentence.

My mother always asks me to _____ the silverware if there are guests coming.

Answer: *burnish*

but.tress [ˈbʌtrəs] n. a projecting structure of masonr

rhyming memory sound –ess

host.ess n. a woman who entertains socially

stew.ar.dess n. a woman who works as a steward

Grammar Tips: -buttressed, -buttressing,

-buttresses, -buttress v., buttressed adj.

Synonym: anchor

Sentence Completion: choose one rhyming word above to complete the sentence.

After the wall collapsed, the construction company agreed to rebuild it with a _____.

Answer: *buttress*

C

ca.co.phony [kəˈkɑfəni] n. harsh or unpleasant nois

rhyming memory sound –ophony

colophony *n.* rosin

ho.mo.phony *n.* of or relating to homophones

Grammar Tips: -cacophonies. *pl.*

Synonym: noise

Sentence Completion: choose one rhyming word above to complete the sentence.

Drawing sensible conclusions is harder still in India where national issues are all but drowned out in a_____of local politics.

Answer: *cacophony*

cajole [kəˈdʒoʊl] v. to coax; to persuade   *rhyming memory sound –ole*

loop.hole *n.* a means of escape;

pa.role *n.* a conditional release of a prisoner

Grammar Tips: -joled, -joling, -joles,

-cajolement *n.* –cajoler *n.* ,   cajolery *n.*

Synonym: coax

Sentence Completion: choose one rhyming word above to complete the sentence.

I'm sure the boy is not guilty; how can we_____your father out of punishing him?

Answer: *cajole*

ca.li.ber [ˈkælɪbər] *n.* degree of worth   *rhyming memory sound –iber/ibber*

jib.ber *n.* one who refuses to proceed further

Grammar Tips: -calibers *pl.*

Synonym: quality

Sentence Completion: choose one rhyming word above to complete the sentence.

He was a man of_____, strength, and character.

Answer: *caliber*

ca.lum.niate [kəˈlʌmnieit] v. to accuse falsely; to slander

rhyming memory sound –iate

con.ci.liate *n.* to gain (as goodwill) by pleasing acts

de.pre.ciate *n.* to lower in estimation or esteem

Grammar Tips: -calumniated, -calumniating, -calunniation *n.*, -calumny *n.*

Synonym: asperse

Sentence Completion: choose one rhyming word above to complete the sentence.

It is usually illegal to_____ the Head of State or President of a country.

Answer: *calumniate*

ca.pri.cious [kəˈprɪʃəs] adj. erratic; impulsive

rhyming memory sound –icious

aus.pi.cious *n.* having favourable prospects; promising

ma.li.cious *n.* showing malice

Grammar Tips: capriciously *adv.*,

–**capriciousness** *n.*, **-caprice** *n.*

Synonym: fickle

Sentence Completion: choose one rhyming word above to complete the sentence.

He was an indecisive sort of person and always_____.

Answer: *capricious*

chaos [ˈkeɪˌɑs] *n.* complete disorder

rhyming memory sound –os

ethos *n.* the set of attitudes and beliefs that are typical of an organization or a group of people

pathos *n.* a quality in a person or situation that makes you feel sad or sorry for them

Grammar Tips: -**chaotic** *adj.*, -**chaotically** *adv.*

Synonym: disorder

Sentence Completion: choose one rhyming word above to complete the sentence.

Economic and political_____might follow – at least, for a time.

Answer: *chaos*

clau.stro.pho.bia [ˌklɔstrəˈfoʊbiə] n. fear of enclosed spaces   *rhyming memory sound –obia*

a.gro.pho.bia *n.* a fear of being in open or public places

xe.no.pho.bia *n.* fear or hatred of foreigners or strangers

Grammar Tips: -**claustrophobic** *adj.*, -**claustrophobe** *n.*

Synonym: n/a

Sentence Completion: choose one rhyming word above to complete the sentence.

The little girl doesn't go in elevators alone because of her _____.

                                            Answer: *claustrophobia*

cle.men.cy ['klemənsi] *n.* mercy; leniency   *rhyming memory sound –ency*

a.gen.cy n. the relationship between a principal and that person's agent

re.si.den.cy n. a state or period of residence

Grammar Tips: -clemencies

                                            Synonym: mercy

Sentence Completion: choose one rhyming word above to complete the sentence.

The Chief of Justice finally decided to show_____to the truly repentant embezzler.

                                            Answer: *clemency*

co.gent [ˈkoʊdʒənt] *adj.* intellectually convincing

rhyming memory sound –ent

aug.ment *n.* to make greater, more numerous, larger, or more

cir.cum.vent *n.* to hem in; to manage to get around by ingenuity

Grammar Tips: -cogently *adv.*

Synonym: compelling

Sentence Completion: choose one rhyming word above to complete the sentence.

This is one attempt to present a comprehensive and_____taxonomy of business models observable on the web.

Answer: *cogent*

co.he.rent [koʊˈhɪrənt] *adj.* logically connected; consistent

rhyming memory sound –erent

ad.he.rent *adj.* able to adhere

in.he.rent *adj.* belonging by nature; involved in the constitution of something

Grammar Tips: -coherently *adv.*

Synonym: logical

Sentence Completion: choose one rhyming word above to complete the sentence.

International policymakers should be asking if these economic realities can be pulled together into a new and_____strategy for change.

Answer: *coherent*

con.co.mi.tant [kənˈkɑmɪtənt] adj. accompanying; attending *rhyming memory sound –itant*

ex.ci.tant *n.* tending to excite or augment

in.ci.tant *n.* to move to action

Grammar Tips: -concomitantly *adv.*

Synonym: accompanying

Sentence Completion: choose one rhyming word above to complete the sentence.

Thermal pollution is an inevitable_____of power generation—an unavoidable implication of the second law of thermodynamics.

Answer: *concomitant*

con.flag.ra.tion [ˌkɑnfləˈgreɪʃ(ə)n] *n.* a large and destructive fire   *rhyming memory sound –ation*

ab.di.ca.tion *n.* giving up a throne, position or power

vin.di.ca.tion *n.* an act of vindicating

Grammar Tips: - conflagrations

Synonym: fire

Sentence Completion: choose one rhyming word above to complete the sentence.

Cool heads and a sense of proportion can yet stop a global trade_____ catching hold.

Answer: *conflagration*

con.ten.tious [kənˈtenʃəs] *adj.* ready to argue; quarrelsome   *rhyming memory sound –entious*

li.cen.tious *adj.* lacking legal or moral restraints

sen.ten.tious *adj.* terse, aphoristic, or moralistic in expression

Grammar Tips: -**contentiously** *adv.*, -**contentiousness** *n.*

Synonym: aggressive

Sentence Completion: choose one rhyming word above to complete the sentence.

The exact nature of these penalties remains just as _____ as many other details.

Answer: *contentious*

con.ti.guous [kən'tɪgjuəs] adj. nearby; neighboring

rhyming memory sound –uous

am.bi.guous *n.* capable of being subject to several interpretations

ex.i.guous *n.* excessively scanty

Grammar Tips: -**contiguously** *adv.*, -**contiguousness** *n.*

Synonym: abutting

Sentence Completion: choose one rhyming word above to complete the sentence.

Multiple_____ cells within a table can be combined into a single cell.

Answer: *contiguous*

con.tra.vene [ˌkɑntrəˈvin] *v.* to go against; to oppose

rhyming memory sound –ene

con.vene *n.* to summon before a tribunal

su.per.vene *n.* to occur as something additional, adventitious, or unexpected

Grammar Tips: -vened, -vening, -venes;

-contravener *n.*

Synonym: breach

Sentence Completion: choose one rhyming word above to complete the sentence.

French publishers also claim the agreement will_____laws in their homeland.

Answer: *contravene*

con.trite [ˈkɑnˌtraɪt] *adj.* sorrowful; penitent   ***rhyming memory sound –ite***

re.spite *n.* a period of temporary delay

re.con.dite *n.* not easily understood

Grammar Tips: -**contritely** *adv.*, -**contriteness** *n.*

                                                        Synonym: apologetic

Sentence Completion: choose one rhyming word above to complete the sentence.

His_____ tears moved his mother, but made his father even more angry.

                                                   Answer: *contrite*

con.ven.tion.al [kənˈvenʃ(ə)nəl] *adj.* relating to general acceptance of practices or attitudes   ***rhyming memory sound –entional***

in.ten.tion.al *adj.* done by intention or design

pre.ven.tion.al *adj.* act of preventing

Grammar Tips: -**conventionally** *adv.*, -**conventionalism** *n.*, -**conventionalist** *n.*, -**conventionalize** *v.*

                                                   Synonym: standard

Sentence Completion: choose one rhyming word above to complete the sentence.

To define such widely spread misconceptions, Galbraith wrote: "I shall refer to these ideas henceforth as the_____wisdom."

Answer: *conventional*

cre.du.li.ty [krəˈdjulǝti] *n.* readiness to believe; gullibility

rhyming memory sound –ulity

gar.ru.li.ty *n.* the quality or state of being garrulous

se.du.li.ty *n.* sedulous activity

Grammar Tips: -credulous *adj.*

Synonym: gullibility

Sentence Completion: choose one rhyming word above to complete the sentence.

The system takes advantage of their opportunism and_____to collect money for the government and to enrich the few.

Answer: *credulity*

cul.pable [ˈkʌlpəb(ə)l] *adj.* blameworthy *rhyming memory sound –able*

un.stable n. not steady in action or movement

ther.mo.stable n. stable when heated

Grammar Tips: -**culpability** *n.*, -**culpableness** *n.*, -**culpably** *adv.*

Synonym: blamable

Sentence Completion: choose one rhyming word above to complete the sentence.

At first, he could not get rid of a_____sense of license on his part.

Answer: *culpable*

cu.mu.la.tive [ˈkjumjələtɪv] *adj.* collected; accumulated

rhyming memory sound –ative

ag.gre.ga.tive *adj.* of or relating to an aggregate

co.gi.ta.tive *n.* of or relating to cogitation

Grammar Tips: - **cumulatively** *adv.*, - **cumulativeness** *n.*

Synonym: accretive

Sentence Completion: choose one rhyming word above to complete the sentence.

The _____ result of these efforts is the healthy and sustained business growth in the last five years.

Answer: *cumulative*

cu.pi.di.ty [kjuˈpɪdəti] n. greed, strong desire   *rhyming memory sound –idity*

a.ri.di.ty n. excessively dry

tur.gi.di.ty n. being in a state of distension

Grammar Tips: -cupidities *pl.*

Synonym: avarice

Sentence Completion: choose one rhyming word above to complete the sentence.

It certainly was not worth while to throw a veil of innocence over such palpable human _____.

Answer: *cupidity*

cur.so.ry [ˈkɜrsəri] *adj.* superficial; hasty   *rhyming memory sound –ory*

sen.so.ry adj. of or relating to sensation

sta.tu.to.ry adj. of or relating to statutes

Grammar Tips: - **cursorily** *adv.*, - **cursoriness** *n.*

                                                   Synonym: hasty

Sentence Completion: choose one rhyming word above to complete the sentence.

This then is something of a_____view of the direction taken by contemporary quantum field theory.

                                                   Answer: *cursory*

D

de.ci.bel [ˈdesɪˌbel] n. a unit for measuring the loudness of sounds *rhyming memory sound -el*

ca.ra.vel n. any of several sailing ships

ci.ta.del n. a fortress that commands a city

Grammar Tips: -decibels *pl.*

Synonym: babel

Sentence Completion: choose one rhyming word above to complete the sentence.

The noise pollution has reached a high_____level.

Answer: *decibel*

de.ci.duous [dɪˈsɪdʒuəs] *adj.* not permanent; passing

rhyming memory sound −uous

ar.duous *adj.* hard to accomplish or achieve

as.si.duous *adj.* marked by careful unremitting attention

Grammar Tips: -deciduousness *n.*

Synonym: *ephemeral*

Sentence Completion: choose one rhyming word above to complete the sentence.

The importance of this field is emphasized by the fact that over half of the _____ fruits produced are processed.

Answer: *deciduous*

de.cry [dɪˈkraɪ] *v.* to criticize openly, speak out against

rhyming memory sound −y

wry *adj.* bent or twisted in shape or condition; dryly humorous

amp.li.fy *n.* to make larger or greater

Grammar Tips: -cried, -crying

Synonym: *depreciate*

Sentence Completion: choose one rhyming word above to complete the sentence.

Rising nations may_____US imperialism and European meddling and resent the west's innate sense of its own superiority.

Answer: *decry*

de.file [dɪˈfaɪl] *v.* to pollute; to corrupt   *rhyming memory sound –ile*

vile *adj.* not conforming to a high moral standard

be.guile *v.* to attract or delight as if by magic

Grammar Tips: -filed, -filing, -files, -defilement *n.*

–defiler *n.*

Synonym: befoul

Sentence Completion: choose one rhyming word above to complete the sentence.

Do not_____the land where you live and where I dwell, for I, the LORD, dwell among the Israelites.

Answer: *defile*

de.le.terious [ˌdeləˈtɪriəs] *adj.* harmful   *rhyming memory sound –erious*

im.perious adj. fond of ordering people around

mys.terious adj. being beyond one's powers to know, understand, or explain

Grammar Tips: -deleteriously *adv.*

Synonym: adverse

Sentence Completion: choose one rhyming word above to complete the sentence.

But the financial effects can be _____, which seems to be the unintended consequences of the Fed's new policy.

Answer: *deleterious*

de.mur [dɪˈmɜr] v. to present an opposing opinion
rhyming memory sound –ur

con.cur v. to express agreement

in.cur v. to become liable or subject to

Grammar Tips: -murred, -murring, -murs

Synonym: expostulate

Sentence Completion: choose one rhyming word above to complete the sentence.

Business travelers may still _____, but investors are rushing to jump aboard Chinese aircraft.

Answer: *demur*

de.mure [dɪˈmjʊr] *adj.* quiet, modest, reserved, shy

rhyming memory sound –ure

ab.jure *n.* to renounce upon oath

pro.cure *n.* to get possession of

Grammar Tips: -murer, -murest

Synonym: coquettish

Sentence Completion: choose one rhyming word above to complete the sentence.

To counterbalance the hairdo, Tymoshenko's outfits needed to be_____yet commanding.

Answer: *demure*

de.ni.grate [ˈdenɪˌgreɪt] v. to ruin the reputation of

rhyming memory sound –ate

ab.di.cate v. to renounce a throne, high office, dignity, or function

re.pu.diate v. to refuse to have anything to do with

Grammar Tips: -grates, -grating, -grated; -denegation n., denigrative adj., –denigrator n., denigratory adj.

Synonym: belittle

Sentence Completion: choose one rhyming word above to complete the sentence.

The line is clever, but it unfairly_____the predictive power of stock markets.

Answer: *denigrates*

dep.lete [dɪˈplit] v. to use up gradually (resources, strength, etc) *rhyming memory sound –ete*

rep.lete adj. fully or abundantly provided for or filled

sec.rete v. to produce a liquid such as saliva

Grammar Tips: -depletabel *adj.*, -depleter *n.*, -depletion *n.*, -depletive *adj.*

Synonym: exhaust

Sentence Completion: choose one rhyming word above to complete the sentence.

Stress may_____vitamin C in your body, as can smoking, drinking and a variety of drugs, not excepting aspirin.

Answer: *deplete*

de.pre.cate ['deprə,keɪt] *v.* to belittle; to disapprove of

rhyming memory sound –ate

ag.gra.vate *v.* to make worse, more serious, or more severe

per.pe.tuate *v.* to make perpetual or cause to last indefinitely

Grammar Tips: -cates, -cating, -cated

Synonym: decry

Sentence Completion: choose one rhyming word above to complete the sentence.

Some pacifists and all militarists _____ social and political conflicts.

Answer: *deprecate*

de.re.lict ['derəlɪkt] *adj.* abandoned; *n.* a vagrant

rhyming memory sound –ict

con.strict *v.* to stultify, stop, or cause to falter

re.tro.dict *v.* to utilize present information or ideas to infer or explain

Grammar Tips: –derelicts *pl.*

Synonym: negligent

Sentence Completion: choose one rhyming word above to complete the sentence.

It was a decaying building in a dying neighborhood, inhabited, you felt, only by doomed old men and _____ young men.

Answer: *derelict*

de.se.crate ['desəˌkreɪt] *v.* to damage a holy place

rhyming memory sound –ate

dis.si.pate v. to cause to spread thin or scatter and gradually vanish

re.mon.strate v. to present and urge reasons in opposition

Grammar Tips: -crates, crating, -crated;

-**desecrater** or -**desecrator** n.

Synonym: defile

Sentence Completion: choose one rhyming word above to complete the sentence.

I will turn my face away from them, and they will_____my treasured place; robbers will enter it and desecrate it.

Answer: *desecrate*

de.sic.cate [dɛsɪket] v. to dry up; to wither   *rhyming memory sound –ate*

im.mo.late v. to kill or destroy often by fire

tran.sub.stan.tiate v. to change into another substance

Grammar Tips: -cated, -cating, -cates;

-**desiccation** n., -**desiccative** adj. -**desiccator** n

Synonym: dehydrate

Sentence Completion: choose one rhyming word above to complete the sentence.

After the king died, his face started to_____ very quickly, and, strangely enough, his hair came off like dry leaves.

Answer: *desiccate*

de.sul.tory [ˈdes(ə)lˌtɔri] *adj.* wandering from subject to subject   ***rhyming memory sound –ory***

al.le.gory *n.* a symbolic representation

pur.ga.tory *n.* an intermediate state after death for expiatory purification

Grammar Tips: -desultorily *adj.*, -desultoriness *n.*

Synonym: arbitrary

Sentence Completion: choose one rhyming word above to complete the sentence.

She received him in a little parlor: a small unspeckled bower, ornamented with a_____foliage of tissue paper.

Answer: *desultory*

dex.te.ri.ty [dekˈsterəti] *n.* skill; cleverness   *rhyming memory sound –erity*

al.te.ri.ty *n.* otherness; the quality of being radically alien to the conscious self

te.me.ri.ty *n.* unreasonable or foolhardy contempt of danger or opposition

Grammar Tips: Latin origin: *dexteritas*

Synonym: adroitness

Sentence Completion: choose one rhyming word above to complete the sentence.

Increased_____is based on the notion that a jack-of-all-trades is often the master of none.

Answer: *dexterity*

di.a.pha.nous [daɪˈæfənəs] *adj.* light, airy, transparent

rhyming memory sound –ous

dex.te.rous *adj.* mentally adroit and skillful

u.na.ni.mous *adj.* being of one mind

Grammar Tips: -diaphanously *adv.* -diaphanousness *n.*

Synonym: transparent

Sentence Completion: choose one rhyming word above to complete the sentence.

She wore a _____ garment at the reunion last night.

Answer: *diaphanous*

di.cho.to.my [daɪˈkɑtəmi] *n.* division into two parts

rhyming memory sound –otomy

hys.te.ro.to.my *n.* surgical incision of the uterus

la.pa.ro.to.my *n.* surgical incision of the abdominal wall

Grammar Tips: -dichotomies *pl.*

Synonym: contradiction

Sentence Completion: choose one rhyming word above to complete the sentence.

Mr Obama played up the _____ between corporations that have returned to profitability and still-struggling smaller businesses.

Answer: *dichotomy*

dic.tion [ˈdɪkʃ(ə)n] *n.* style of speaking *rhyming memory sound -iction*

con.stric.tion *n.* an act or product of constricting

ju.ris.dic.tion *n.* the power, right, or authority to interpret and apply the law

Grammar Tips: -*dictional adj.*, -*dictionally adv.*

Synonym: articulation

Sentence Completion: choose one rhyming word above to complete the sentence.

Bad _____ marred the effectiveness of her speech.

Answer: *diction*

dif.fi.dent [ˈdɪfɪdənt] *adj.* shy; modest *rhyming memory sound –ent*

cir.cum.vent *v.* to manage to get around by ingenuity

coin.ci.dent *adj.* occupying the same space or time

Grammar Tips: -diffidently *adv.*

Synonym: coy

Sentence Completion: choose one rhyming word above to complete the sentence.

Dick was always_____when it came to staff matters, and not been able to summon up the gumption to bang the table.

Answer: *diffident*

dis.cur.sive [dɪsˈkɜrsɪv] *adj.* rambling; wandering

rhyming memory sound –ursive

ex.cur.sive *adj.* constituting a digression

re.cur.sive *adj.* involving a process that continues to be repeated again and again

Grammar Tips: -discursively *adv.,* **-discursiveness** *n.*

Synonym: desultory

Sentence Completion: choose one rhyming word above to complete the sentence.

As the lecturer wandered from topic to topic, we wandered what if any point there was to his _____ remarks.

                                                Answer: *discursive*

dis.semble [dɪˈsemb(ə)l] v. to conceal; to pretend

rhyming memory sound –emble

as.semble *n.* to fit together the parts of

re.semble *n.* to be like or similar to

Grammar Tips: -sembles, -sembling, -sembled; -dissembler *n.*

                                                 Synonym: feign

Sentence Completion: choose one rhyming word above to complete the sentence.

She tried to _____ her anger with a smile on her face.

                                                Answer: *dissemble*

di.ther [ˈdɪðər] v. to be indecisive, nervously confused

rhyming memory sound –ither

sli.ther *v.* to slide on or as if on a loose gravelly surface

wi.ther *v.* to become dry and sapless

Grammar Tips: -dithers, -dithering, dithered, -dither *n.*

Synonym: hesitate

Sentence Completion: choose one rhyming word above to complete the sentence.

Instead, like the rest of Washington, it's inventing reasons to _____ in the face of mass unemployment.

Answer: *dither*

du.pli.ci.ty [duˈplɪsəti] *n.* deceit; double-dealing

rhyming memory sound –icity

e.las.ti.ci.ty *n.* the quality or state of being elastic

syn.chro.ni.ci.ty *n.* the quality or fact of being synchronous

Grammar Tips: -duplicities *pl.* -duplicity theory *n.*

Synonym: artifice

Sentence Completion: choose one rhyming word above to complete the sentence.

She was suspicious that her boss was guilty of_____in his private dealings.

Answer: *duplicity*

E

e.bul.lient [ɪˈbʊljənt] adj. enthusiastic   *rhyming memory sound –lient*

le.nient *adj.* of mild and tolerant disposition

re.si.lient *adj.* able to quickly become healthy, happy, or strong again

after an illness, disappointment, or other problem

Grammar Tips: -ebulliently *adv.,*-ebullience *n.*

Synonym: agitated

Sentence Completion: choose one rhyming word above to complete the sentence.

He was terribly nervous and extremely jealous and he covered his nervous jealousy with an_____friendliness.

Answer: *ebullient*

e.clipse [ɪˈklɪps] *v.* to overshadow; to outshine

rhyming memory sound –ipse

e.llipse *n.* oval; a shape similar to a circle but longer than it is wide

to.tal ec.lipse *n.* an eclipse in which all of the Sun or Moon is covered

Grammar Tips: -lipses, -lipsing, -lipsed; eclipse *n.*

Synonym: surpass

Sentence Completion: choose one rhyming word above to complete the sentence.

If one were to draw the correct historical analogy, the potential_____of the dollar is just a decade away

Answer: *eclipse*

ec.sta.tic [ɪkˈstætɪk] *adj.* extremely happy   *rhyming memory sound –atic*

schis.ma.tic *n.* one who creates or takes part in schism

sci.a.tic *adj.* of, relating to, or situated near the hip

Grammar Tips: -ecstatically *adv.*,

-ecstatics *n.*, -ecstacy *n.*

Synonym: elated

Sentence Completion: choose one rhyming word above to complete the sentence.

As his teammates sprinted to smother him in an _____ scrum, several Ghanaians slumped to the field.

Answer: *ecstatic*

ef.fi.ca.cy ['efɪkəsi] *n.* power to produce an effect

rhyming memory sound –acy

de.li.cacy *n.* the quality or state of being luxurious

tes.tacy *n.* the state of being testate

Grammar Tips: -efficacies *pl..*

Synonym: edge

Sentence Completion: choose one rhyming word above to complete the sentence.

Mr. Cameron is said to be deeply sceptical about the purpose and_____of the war in Afghanistan

Answer: *efficacy*

ef.fi.gy ['efɪdʒi] *n.* a likeness; an image **rhyming memory sound –y**

stin.gy *adj.* not generous or liberal

e.le.gy *n.* a poem in elegiac couplets

Grammar Tips: -effigies *pl..*

Synonym: image

Sentence Completion: choose one rhyming word above to complete the sentence.

There the_____stands, and stares from age to age across the changing ocean.

Answer: *effigy*

ef.fron.te.ry [ɪˈfrʌntəri] *n.* shameful boldness

rhyming memory sound –ery

que.ry *n.* a question in the mind : doubt

sphe.ry *n.* having the shape of a sphere

Grammar Tips: *-effronteries pl.*

                                                  Synonym: *audaciousness*

Sentence Completion: choose one rhyming word above to complete the sentence.

The _____ of that may well supersede anything Goldman and Paulson are alleged to have done.

                                                  Answer: *effrontery*

e.gre.gious [ɪˈgridʒəs] *adj.* remarkably bad; outrageous

rhyming memory sound –ious

du.bious *adj.* of doubtful promise or outcome

te.dious *adj.* tiresome because of length or dullness

Grammar Tips: *-egregiously adv., -egregiousness n.*

                                                  Synonym: *blatant*

Sentence Completion: choose one rhyming word above to complete the sentence.

No other supplier of any other service would even dare to behave in such an _____ and cavalier manner.

Answer: *egregious*

e.gress ['iˌgres] *v.* to exit   *rhyming memory sound –ess*

o.bsess *v.* to worry about something all the time

re.gress *v.* to go back to a previous and usually lower state or level

Grammar Tips: -gresses, -gressing, -gressed

Synonym: exit

Sentence Completion: choose one rhyming word above to complete the sentence.

I am like the cat plying on the _____, trying to seizing this cunning mouse even though out of reach now.

Answer: *egress*

e.la.bo.rate [ɪˈlæb(ə)rət] *n.* to work out with precision, in full detail

rhyming memory sound -ate

ab.ne.gate *v.* to give up or renounce something

ag.gre.gate *v.* to add amounts together; to put things together in a group

Grammar Tips: -elaborate *adj.* -elaboration *n.*

Synonym: develop

Sentence Completion: choose one rhyming word above to complete the sentence.

Mr. Holleyman declined to _____ on how much more common he thought they might become.

Answer: *elaborate*

em.pa.thy [ˈempəθi] *n.* understanding another's feelings

rhyming memory sound –athy

al.le.lo.pa.thy *n.* the release into the environment by one plant of a substance that inhibits the germination of other potential competitor plants of the same or another species

te.le.pa.thy *n.* the ability of people to communicate directly with each other's minds, without using words

Grammar Tips: -empathetic *adj.*, -empathetically *adv.*,

-empathic *adj.*, -empathically *adv.*

Synonym: compassion

Sentence Completion: choose one rhyming word above to complete the sentence.

Human factors in design used to be about having_____for the individual and their relationship with a product, that's where it started.

Answer: *empathy*

en.cum.brance [ɪnˈkʌmbrəns] *n.* hindrance; obstruction

rhyming memory sound –ance

as.kance *adv.* with distrust

per.chance *adv.* it is possible

Grammar Tips: -encumbrances *pl.*

Synonym: deterrent

Sentence Completion: choose one rhyming word above to complete the sentence.

The woman deserted her little child because she regarded him as her_____.

Answer: *encumbrance*

endemic [ɪnˈkʌmbrəns] *adj.* confined to a particular country or area *rhyming memory sound–emic*

epiemic *adj.* exciting a similar feeling or reaction in others
epistemic *adj.* relating to knowledge

Grammar Tips: -endemics *pl.*, -endemic *n.*

Synonym: aboriginal

Sentence Completion: choose one rhyming word above to complete the sentence.

A hot climate_____people who are not used to it.

Answer: *endemic*

e.ner.vate [ˈɛnɚˌvet] *v.* to weaken, exhaust   *rhyming memory sound –ate*

be.rate *v.* to criticize (someone) severely or angrily

con.flate *n.* to combine two or more things

Grammar Tips: -vated, vating, vates.

                                      Synonym: debilitate

Sentence Completion: choose one rhyming word above to complete the sentence.

A hot climate_____people who are not used to it.

                                      Answer: *enervates*

e.nig.ma [ɪˈnɪgmə] *n.* a puzzling situation; dilemma

rhyming memory sound –igma

sig.ma *n.* the 18th letter of the Greek alphabet, represented in the English alphabet as 's'

stig.ma *n.* a mark of shame or discredit

Grammar Tips: - enigmas *pl.*

                                      Synonym: conundrum

Sentence Completion: choose one rhyming word above to complete the sentence.

Well, you're a mystery for her just like she's an_____for you.

Answer: *enigma*

en.nui [ɑnˈwi] *n.* boredom   *rhyming memory sound –ui*

e.tui *n.* a small ornamental case

point d'ap.pui *n.* point of support

Grammar Tips: from old French: **enui**.

Synonym: boredom

Sentence Completion: choose one rhyming word above to complete the sentence.

It is aging and losing competitiveness. And a general_____is creeping through society.

Answer: *ennui*

en.sconce [ɪnˈskɑns] *v.* to hide; to conceal; to settle comfortably   *rhyming memory sound –once*

nonce *n.* the one, particular, or present occasion, purpose, or use

sconce *n.* a bracket candlestick or group of candlesticks

Grammar Tips: -conces, -concing, -conced

Synonym: lodge

Sentence Completion: choose one rhyming word above to complete the sentence.

Against that time do I_____here.

Answer: *ensconce*

e.phe.me.ral [ɪˈfem(ə)rəl] *adj.* temporary; short-lived

rhyming memory sound –al

fe.ral *adj.* not domesticated or cultivated

se.ral *adj.* of, relating to, or constituting an ecological sere

Grammar Tips: -ephemeral *n.* ephemerals *pl.*.

Synonym: deciduous

Sentence Completion: choose one rhyming word above to complete the sentence.

Some Japanese say that the cherry blossom's_____nature serves as a poignant reminder of how life itself is fleeting.

Answer: *ephemeral*

e.pi.gram ['epɪˌgræm] *n.* witty saying   *rhyming memory sound –am*

chro.no.gram *n.* an inscription or phrase in which certain letters express a date or epoch

cryp.to.gram *n.* a communication in cipher or code

Grammar Tips: -epigrams *pl.*, -epigrammatism *n.*,

-epigrammatist *n.*

Synonym: aphorism

Sentence Completion: choose one rhyming word above to complete the sentence.

An_____is a half-truth so stated as to irritate the person who believes the other half.

Answer: *epigram*

e.pi.taph ['epɪˌtæf] *n.* inscription on a tomb   *rhyming memory sound –aph*

cryp.to.graph *n.* a system of secret or cipher writing; a cipher.

seis.mo.graph *n.* an instrument that is used for measuring the strength of earthquakes

Grammar Tips: -**epitaphial** *adj.*,

-**epitaphic** *adj.*, -**epitaphs** *pl.*

Synonym: n/a

Sentence Completion: choose one rhyming word above to complete the sentence.

Believe a woman or an_____, or any other thing that's false, before you trust in critics.

Answer: *epitaph*

e.qua.ni.mi.ty [ˌekwəˈnɪməti] *n.* calmness; evenness of temperament   *rhyming memory sound –imity*

sub.li.mi.ty *n.* the quality or state of being sublime

pu.sil.la.ni.mi.ty *n.* the quality or state of being pusillanimous

Grammar Tips: Latin origin: **aequanimita**

Synonym: tranquility

Sentence Completion: choose one rhyming word above to complete the sentence.

If it does, one can contemplate the prospective jump in government explicit and contingent debt with_____.

Answer: *equanimity*

e.ru.dite ['erə,daɪt] *adj.* scholarly; learned   *rhyming memory sound –ite*

tri.par.tite *adj.* divided into or composed of three parts

re.con.dite *adj.* requiring a high degree of scholarship or specialist knowledge to be understood

Grammar Tips: Latin origin: **eruditus**

Synonym: knowledgeable

Sentence Completion: choose one rhyming word above to complete the sentence.

You may read scores of_____tomes on psychology without coming across a statement more significant for you and for me.

Answer: *erudite*

es.chew [esˈtʃu] *v.* to avoid; to keep away from

rhyming memory sound –ew

as.kew *adv.* or *adj.* out of line : awry

cur.few *n.* a law that does not allow people to go outside between a

particular time in the evening and a particular time in the morning

Grammar Tips: -chews, -chewing, -chewed;
-eschewal *n.*

Synonym: avoid

Sentence Completion: choose one rhyming word above to complete the sentence.

You may read scores of _____ tomes on psychology without coming across a statement more significant for you and for me.

Answer: *erudite*

e.so.te.ric [ˌesəˈterɪk] *adj.* for a select few; not generally known   *rhyming memory sound –eric*

ge.ne.ric *adj.* relating to or having the rank of a biological genus

bi.os.pheric *adj.* the part of the world in which life can exist

Grammar Tips: - **esoterically** *adv.*

Synonym: abstruse

Sentence Completion: choose one rhyming word above to complete the sentence.

Finance is not a mysterious or _____ subject, but it is often misunderstood.

Answer: *esoteric*

eu.lo.gy [ˈjulədʒi] *n.* praise for a dead person   *rhyming memory sound –ogy*

neu.ro.lo.gy *n.* the scientific study of the nervous system especially in respect to its structures, functions, and abnormalities

e.pis.te.mo.lo.gy *n.* the study or a theory of the nature and grounds of knowledge especially with reference to its limits and validity

Grammar Tips: - **eulogies** *pl.*

Synonym: accolade

Sentence Completion: choose one rhyming word above to complete the sentence.

I wondered too, after reading the_____, if I was right to infer that Jobs saw something, and if so, what did he see?

Answer: *eulogy*

eu.phe.mism [ˈjufəˌmɪzəm] *n.* substitution of a more pleasant expression   ***rhyming memory sound –ism***

a.nar.chism *n.* the advocacy or practice of anarchistic principles

a.pho.rism *n.* a concise statement of a principle

Grammar Tips: **-euphemisms** *pl.*, **-euphemist** *n.*, **-euphemistic** *adj.* **-euphemistically** *adv.*

Synonym: n/a

Sentence Completion: choose one rhyming word above to complete the sentence.

The European Commission calls it a "stability bond", surely a candidate for_____of the year.

Answer: *euphemism*

eu.pho.nious [juːˈfəʊniəs] *adj.* having a pleasant sound;

harmonious   *rhyming memory sound –onious*

par.s.i.mo.nious *adj.* not willing to give or spend money

sanc.ti.mo.nious *adj.* hypocritically pious or devout

Grammar Tips:-**euphoniously** *adv.*, -**euphoniousness** *n.*

Synonym: lyrical

Sentence Completion: choose one rhyming word above to complete the sentence.

Prescott's style, though in his diary he wrote "bother euphony", is _____.

Answer: *euphonious*

eu.pho.ria [juˈfɔriə] *n.* a feeling of well-being

rhyming memory sound –oria

dys.pho.ria *n.* a state of feeling unwell or unhappy

phan.tas.ma.go.ria *n.* an exhibition of optical effects and illusions

Grammar Tips:-**euphoric** *adj.*, -**euphorically** *adv.*

Synonym: cloud nine

Sentence Completion: choose one rhyming word above to complete the sentence.

The initial **euphoria** lasts a few weeks, a few days or even just a few hours—and the cycle begins once again.

Answer: euphoria

eu.tha.na.sia [ˌjuθəˈneɪʒə] *n.* mercy killing   *rhyming memory sound –asia*

fan.ta.sia *n.* a work (as a poem or play) in which the author's fancy roves unrestricted

pa.ro.no.ma.sia *n.* a play on words : pun

Grammar Tips:- **euthanastic** *adj.*

Synonym: n/a

Sentence Completion: choose one rhyming word above to complete the sentence.

_____, or "mercy killing," is legal only in the Netherlands, Luxembourg, Belgium, and the US state of Oregon.

Answer: Euthanasia

e.va.nes.cent [ˌevəˈnes(ə)nt] *adj.* temporary; fleeting

rhyming memory sound –escent

a.cqui.escent *adj.* inclined to acquiesce

con.va.lescent *adj.* recovering health and strength gradually after sickness or weakness

Grammar Tips: Latin origin: **evanescent**

Synonym: brief

Sentence Completion: choose one rhyming word above to complete the sentence.

The joy and moral stimulation of work no longer must be forgotten in the mad chase of _____ profits.

Answer: *evanescent*

e.vince [ɪˈvɪns] *v.* to show clearly *rhyming memory sound –ince*

quince *n,* the fruit of a central Asian tree

wince *v.* to shrink back involuntarily (as from pain) : flinch

Grammar Tips: -vinces, -vincing, -vinced

Synonym: bespeak

Sentence Completion: choose one rhyming word above to complete the sentence.

His conversation_____great courage.

Answer: *evinces*

e.xa.cer.bate [ɪgˈzæsərˌbeɪt] *v.* to aggravate; to make more violent   *rhyming memory sound –ate*

sa.tu.rate *v.* to treat, furnish, or charge with something to the point where no more can be absorbed, dissolved, or retained

se.gre.gate *v.* to separate or set apart from others or from the general mass : isolate

Grammar Tips: -bated, -bating, -bates; - exacerbation *n.*

Synonym: aggravate

Sentence Completion: choose one rhyming word above to complete the sentence.

In an environment of this complexity, point solutions merely_____the problem, and will never lead us out of the woods.

Answer: *exacerbate*

e.xas.pe.rate [ɪgˈzæspəˌreɪt] *v.* to irritate; to annoy extremely   *rhyming memory sound –ate*

a.cer.bate *v.* to irritate; to exasperate

cor.re.late *v.* to bear reciprocal or mutual relations

Grammar Tips: -rates, -rating, -rated; **exasperatedly** *adv.,* **exasperatingly** *adv.*

Synonym: annoy

Sentence Completion: choose one rhyming word above to complete the sentence.

Fathers, do not _____ your children; instead, bring them up in the training and instruction of the Lord.

Answer: *exasperate*

ex.cul.pate [ˈekskʌlˌpeɪt] *v.* to free from blame; to vindicate   *rhyming memory sound –ate*

ar.bi.trate *v.* to submit or refer for decision to an arbiter

mi.ti.gate *v.* to cause to become less harsh or hostile : mollify

Grammar Tips: -pates, -pating, -pated;

-**exculpate** *n.* -**exculpation** *n.*

Synonym: acquit

Sentence Completion: choose one rhyming word above to complete the sentence.

He_____himself from a charge of theft.

Answer: *exculpated*

ex.hume [ɪg'zum] *v.* to bring out of the earth; to reveal

rhyming memory sound –ume

pre.sume *v.* to undertake without leave or clear justification

as.sume *v.* to take into partnership, employment, or use

Grammar Tips: -humes, -huming, -humed;

-**exhumation** *n.*, -**exhumer** *n.*

Synonym: unearth

Sentence Completion: choose one rhyming word above to complete the sentence.

The remains of the billionaire were_____in Paris and transported his hometown.

Answer: *exhumed*

e.xi.gent ['eksidʒənt] *adj.* urgent; critical **rhyming memory sound –ent**

a.li.ment *n.* food, nutriment

re.gi.ment *n.* a military unit consisting usually of a number of battalions

Grammar Tips: -exigently *adv.*

Synonym: emergent

Sentence Completion: choose one rhyming word above to complete the sentence.

These surely were the kind of "unusual and_____" circumstances that permit the Fed to take emergency action.

Answer: *exigent*

e.xor.bi.tant [ɪgˈzɔrbɪtənt] *adj.* excessive; unreasonable

rhyming memory sound –ant

co.ve.nant *n.* a usually formal, solemn, and binding agreement

sy.co.phant *n.* a servile self-seeking flatterer

Grammar Tips: - exorbitantly *adv.*

Synonym: baroque

Sentence Completion: choose one rhyming word above to complete the sentence.

This was an "_____ privilege", grumbled France's finance minister at the time, Valéry Giscard d'Estaing.

Answer: *exorbitant*

ex.pi.ate ['ekspi‚eɪt] *v.* to atone for   *rhyming memory sound –iate*

sa.ti.ate *v.* to supply with anything to excess, so as to disgust or weary

sub.stan.ti.ate *v.* to establish by proof or competent evidence

Grammar Tips: -piates, -piating, -piated;

-expiable *adj.* **-expiator** *n.*

Synonym: redeem

Sentence Completion: choose one rhyming word above to complete the sentence.

The latter's yearning to_____a guilt that was in retrospect vastly exaggerated or nonexistent prolonged the war.

Answer: *expiate*

ex.punge [ɪk'spʌndʒ] v. to erase **rhyming memory sound –unge**

grunge *n.* something of inferior quality; trash:

plunge *v.* to bring suddenly or forcibly into some condition, situation, etc.

Grammar Tips: -punges, -punging, -punged; -expunger *n.*, **-expunged** *adj.*

Synonym: erase

Sentence Completion: choose one rhyming word above to complete the sentence.

The juvenile court may_____or destroy the records of a juvenile at any time.

Answer: *expunge*

ex.pur.gate [ˈekspə:geit] v. to remove offensive passages; to cleanse   *rhyming memory sound –ate*

cul.mi.nate v. to reach the highest point, summit, or highest development

re.mon.strate v. to say or plead in protest, objection, or disapproval

Grammar Tips: -**expurgation** n., -**expurgater** n., -**expurgated** adj.

Synonym: delete

Sentence Completion: choose one rhyming word above to complete the sentence.

An _____ edition of a book has had offensive words or descriptions changed or removed.

Answer: *expurgated*

ex.tant [ekˈstænt] adj. still in existence   *rhyming memory sound –ant*

as.lant adj. or adv. in a slanting direction : obliquely

sup.plant v. to supersede (another) especially by force or treachery

Grammar Tips: non-extant *adj.*

Synonym: existent

Sentence Completion: choose one rhyming word above to complete the sentence.

What we have_____right now, at the beginning of this system,

is the U.N. Security Council as a grand jury. What can they do?

Answer: *extant*

ex.tol [ɪk'stoʊl] v. to praise highly   ***rhyming memory sound –ol***

sol n. the Roman god of the sun

cho.les.te.rol n. a substance that is found in the blood and the cells of the body. It can cause diseases of the heart and the arteries if there is too much of it

Grammar Tips: -tols, -tolling, -tolled;

-extoller *n.*, -extolment *n.*

Synonym: glorify

Sentence Completion: choose one rhyming word above to complete the sentence.

Some earlier studies that_____dairy products as a calcium source

have been funded at least in part by the dairy industry.

Answer: *extol*

ex.tra.po.late [ɪkˈstræpəˌleɪt] *v.* to estimate; to infer

rhyming memory sound –ate

fluc.tu.ate *v.* to change frequently

sur.ro.gate *n.* someone or something that replaces another person or thing as their representative

Grammar Tips: -lates, -lating, -lated; - extrapolation *n.*, extrapolative adj., -extrapolator *n.*

Synonym: conclude

Sentence Completion: choose one rhyming word above to complete the sentence.

The best one can do is to try to_____one's pattern of thought from two dimensions to

three and then to four, to form analogies.

Answer: *extrapolate*

F

fa.ce.tious [fə'siʃəs] *adj.* joking; sarcastic   *rhyming memory sound –etious/ecious*

spe.cious *adj.* having a false look of truth or genuineness

ca.pri.cious *adj.* governed or characterized by caprice : impulsive, unpredictable

Grammar Tips: - **facetiously** *adv.*, - **facetiousness** *n.*

Synonym: clever

Sentence Completion: choose one rhyming word above to complete the sentence.

Punning, _____, irreverent, the funny man filled the newspapers and lighter periodicals with his material.

Answer: *facetious*

fal.la.cious [fəˈleɪʃəs] *adj.* misleading; deceptive
rhyming memory sound –acious

sa.ga.cious *adj.* of keen and farsighted penetration and judgment

ve.ra.cio.us *adj.* marked by truth : accurate

Grammar Tips: -fallaciously *adv.*, -fallaciousness *n.*

Synonym: illogical

Sentence Completion: choose one rhyming word above to complete the sentence.

Numerous examples might be cited to support_____claims , but they most often lack a relevance to the issue under discussion.

Answer: *fallacious*

fas.ti.dious [fəˈstɪdiəs] *adj.* hard to please , meticulous
rhyming memory sound –idious

in.si.dious *adj.* awaiting a chance to entrap : treacherous

per.fi.dious *adj.* of, relating to, or characterized by perfidy

Grammar Tips: -fastidiously *adv.*, -fastidiousness *n.*

Synonym: choosy

Sentence Completion: choose one rhyming word above to complete the sentence.

There was also among the Italians of that period a singular and_____apprehension of too much daylight.

Answer: *fastidious*

fa.tuous ['fætʃuəs] *adj.* foolish   *rhyming memory sound –uous*

vir.tuous *adj.* morally excellent : righteous

com.temp.tuous *adj.* expressing extreme contempt

Grammar Tips: -fatuously *adv.*, -fatuousness *n.*

Synonym: airheaded

Sentence Completion: choose one rhyming word above to complete the sentence.

Over the past week or so, the opinion pages of US newspapers have raised this_____ventilation almost to the level of mass hysteria.

Answer: *fatuous*

fea.sible ['fizəb(ə)l] *adj.* capable of being accomplished

rhyming sound –easible

de.fea.sible *adj.* capable of being made or declared null or void

in.fea.sible *adj.* not practical or easily achieved

Grammar Tips: -feasibility *n.,* -feasibly *adj.*

Synonym: possible

Sentence Completion: choose one rhyming word above to complete the sentence.

It is not_____to wait a few days until the body's regulatory mechanisms are used to the new time zone.

Answer: *feasible*

fe.cund ['fekənd] *adj.* fertile; productive   *rhyming memory sound –und*

ob.tund *v.* to reduce the edge or violence of

ru.bi.cund *adj.* ruddy

Grammar Tips: -*fecundity n.*

Synonym: cornucopian

Sentence Completion: choose one rhyming word above to complete the sentence.

The elite student is well noted for his industry and_____ mind.

Answer: *fecund*

flip.pant ['flɪpənt] *adj.* treating serious matters

rhyming memory sound –ant

as.lant *adv.* or *adj.* in a slanting direction : obliquely

re.cant *v.* to withdraw or repudiate (a statement or belief) formally and publicly : renounce

Grammar Tips: - *flippantly adv.*

Synonym: facetious

Sentence Completion: choose one rhyming word above to complete the sentence.

I'm not saying to be _____ in prayer, but that's how you make

contact with God. You just talk with him in a genuine and heartfelt way.

Answer: *flippant*

flo.rid ['flɔrɪd] *adj.* flowery; ornate   **rhyming memory sound –orid/orrid**

hor.rid *adj.* innately offensive or repulsive

tor.rid *adj.* parched with heat especially of the sun

Grammar Tips: -floridity *n.*, -floridly *adv.*, -floridness *n.*

Synonym: ornate

Sentence Completion: choose one rhyming word above to complete the sentence.

His _____ rhetorical style was typical of the era, and that speech is

all but forgotten.

Answer: *florid*

for.tui.tous [fɔr'tuɪtəs] *adj.* lucky; by chance

rhyming memory sound –uitous

cir.cui.tous *adj.* having a circular or winding course

gra.tui.tous *adj.* given unearned or without recompense

Grammar Tips: -fortuitously *adv.*, **-fortuitousness** *n.*

Synonym: fortunate

Sentence Completion: choose one rhyming word above to complete the sentence.

Since the price stability you describe is not matched in other markets,

could it be purely_____?

Answer: *fortuitous*

fri.vo.lous ['frɪvələs] *adj.* trivial; silly *rhyming memory sound –ous*

in.ge.nious *adj.* having or showing an unusual aptitude for discovering, inventing, or contriving

rau.cous *adj.* disagreeably harsh or strident : hoarse

Grammar Tips: *-frivolously adv., -frivolousness n.*

Synonym: fiddling

Sentence Completion: choose one rhyming word above to complete the sentence.

In February, historian Patrick Weber branded the star a '_____fashion victim who is isolated

from reality' in a book about her life.

Answer: *frivolous*

G

gar.ru.lous [ˈgerələs] *adj.* talkative *rhyming memory sound –ulous*

hi.deous *adj.* offensive to the senses and especially to sight : exceedingly ugly

que.ru.lous *adj.* habitually complaining

Grammar Tips: -**garrulously** *adv.*, -**garrulousness** *n.*

Synonym: blabby

Sentence Completion: choose one rhyming word above to complete the sentence.

Miss Thompson, loud-voiced and_____, was evidently quite willing to gossip.

Answer: *garrulous*

gi.gan.tic [dʒaɪˈgæntɪk] *adj.* huge; enormous

rhyming memory sound -antic

ne.cro.man.tic *adj.* given to or produced by or used in the art of conjuring up the dead

sy.co.phan.tic *adj.* attempting to win favor by flattery: dawning; obsequious

Grammar Tips: -gigantically *adv.*

Synonym: colossal

Sentence Completion: choose one rhyming word above to complete the sentence.

All those colors are ice and it goes up to about two miles thick, just a_____dome that comes in from the coast and rises in the middle.

Answer: *gigantic*

gran.di.lo.quent [grænˈdɪləkwənt] *adj.* pretentious

rhyming memory sound –uent

con.fluent *adj.* flowing or coming together

in.con.gruent *adj.* not congruent

Grammar Tips: -**grandiloquently** *adv.*

Synonym: bragging

Sentence Completion: choose one rhyming word above to complete the sentence.

The politician could never speak simply; she was always _____.

Answer: *grandiloquent*

gre.ga.rious [grəˈgeriəs] *adj.* sociable; friendly
rhyming memory sound –arious

pre.ca.rious *adj.* depending on the will or pleasure of another

vi.ca.rious *adj.* serving instead of someone or something else

Grammar Tips: -**gregariously** *adv.*, -**gregariousness** *n.*

Synonym: boon

Sentence Completion: choose one rhyming word above to complete the sentence.

When you're very_____with people, that openness we talked about, the sort of welcoming attitude, some perceive that as very American.

Answer: *gregarious*

H

hack.neyed [ˈhæknid] *adj.* trite; commonplace; overused

rhyming memory sound –ackneyed/acned

ac.ned *adj.* a disorder of the skin caused by inflammation of the skin glands and hair follicles

un.hack.neyed *adj.* being not cliché

Grammar Tips: -hackney *v.*

Synonym: banal

Sentence Completion: choose one rhyming word above to complete the sentence.

Half a century is too long to prepare a two-minute speech, and this one was just a little on the_____side.

Answer: *hackneyed*

hap.ha.zard [hæp'hæzərd] *adj.* dependent upon mere chance   *rhyming memory sound –azard*

ha.zard *n.* a source of danger

at ha.zard *adv.* at stake

Grammar Tips: -haphazardly *adv.*, – haphazardness *n.*

Synonym: random

Sentence Completion: choose one rhyming word above to complete the sentence.

Robert Epstein: Most companies look for new ideas in a kind of _____ way. It's kind of a hope and a prayer, really.

Answer: *haphazard*

hap.less ['hæpləs] *adj.* unlucky   *rhyming memory sound –apless*

sap.less *adj.* having no fluid part (as in plant) or body fluid (as blood)

strap.less *adj.* having no strap

Grammar Tips: -haplessly *adv.*, – haplessness *n.*

Synonym: unlucky

Sentence Completion: choose one rhyming word above to complete the sentence.

The drama in the stocks of banks at the centre of the rumours, with Royal Bank of Scotland the latest_____victim, did not permit that.

Answer: *hapless*

ha.rangue [həˈræŋ] *n.* long speech *rhyming memory sound –angue/ang*

gangue *n.* the worthless rock or vein matter in which valuable metals or minerals occur

slang *n.* language peculiar to a particular group

Grammar Tips: -harangue *v.*

Synonym: tirade

Sentence Completion: choose one rhyming word above to complete the sentence.

After her_____was over and I had been dismissed, the party

continued, but the atmosphere was much more subdued.

Answer: *harangue*

he.ge.mony ['hedʒə,moʊni] *n.* leadership or strong influence   *rhyming memory sound –ony*

sanc.ti.mony *n.* affected or hypocritical holiness

tes.ti.mony *n.* firsthand authentication of a fact

Grammar Tips: -hegemonic *adj.*

Synonym: dominance

Sentence Completion: choose one rhyming word above to complete the sentence.

It was always going to be easier for a US president to climb into the pulpit when Washington felt secure in its_____.

Answer: *hegemony*

hei.nous ['heɪnəs] *adj.* hateful; abominable   *rhyming memory sound –ous*

cal.lous *adj.* being hardened and thickened

hi.deous *adj.* morally offensive

Grammar Tips: -heinously *adv.*, -heinousness *n.*

Synonym: abominable

Sentence Completion: choose one rhyming word above to complete the sentence.

The alleged crimes are _____, evidence of an organization without anything much resembling a moral compass.

Answer: *heinous*

he.te.ro.ge.neous [ˌhetəroʊˈdʒiniəs] *adj.* different; unlike; dissimilar   *rhyming memory sound –eous*

ho.mo.ge.neous *adj.* of the same or a similar kind or nature

mis-cel-la-neous *adj.* consisting of diverse things or members

Grammar Tips: -heterogeneously *adv.*,

-heterogeneousness *n.*

Synonym: miscellaneous

Sentence Completion: choose one rhyming word above to complete the sentence.

It is difficult to imagine such a _____ group finding issues on which their joint interest is at the expense of the global interest.

Answer: *heterogeneous*

hie.rar.chy [ˈhaɪəˌrɑrki] *n.* a ranking, one above the other

rhyming memory sound –archy

a.nar.chy *n.* absence of government

mo.nar.chy *n.* undivided rule or absolute sovereignty by a single person

Grammar Tips: hierarchies *pl.*

Synonym: ranking

Sentence Completion: choose one rhyming word above to complete the sentence.

He added: 'The Earthscraper preserves the iconic presence of the city square and the existin_____ of the buildings that surround it.

Answer: *hierarchy*

ho.mo.ge.neous [ˌhaməˈdʒiniəs] *adj.* composed of parts all of the same kind   *rhyming memory sound –eneous*

he.te.ro.ge.neous *adj.* different; unlike; dissimilar

mis-cel-la-neous *adj.* consisting of diverse things or members

Grammar Tips: -homogeneously *adv.*,

-homogeneousness *n.*

Synonym: n/a

Sentence Completion: choose one rhyming word above to complete the sentence.

We are a racially_____people on the outside, but inside we have become very different as a result of the 63 years of division.

Answer: *homogeneous*

hy.dro.pho.bia [ˌhaidrəˈfəubiə] *n.* fear of water; rabies

rhyming memory sound –obia

a.cro.pho.bia *n.* abnormal dread of being in a high place

xe.no.pho.bia *n.* fear and hatred of strangers or foreigners or of anything that is strange

Grammar Tips: -homogeneously *adv.*, -homogeneousness *n.*

Synonym: n/a

Sentence Completion: choose one rhyming word above to complete the sentence.

_____ will occur and get head even in the coldest weather

Answer: *Hydrophobia*

hy.per.bo.le [haɪˈpɜrbəli] *n.* extreme exaggeration
rhyming memory sound –erbole/erbally

ver.bal.ly *adj.* of, relating to, or consisting of words

non.ver.ba.lly *adj.* not verbal

Grammar Tips: -hyperbolist *n.*

Synonym: caricature

Sentence Completion: choose one rhyming word above to complete the sentence.

In advertising, the term is often used as a_____, a superlative to hype up a product.

Answer: *hyperbole*

hy.po.crite [ˈhɪpəkrɪt] *n.* one who pretends to be what he is not   *rhyming memory sound –ite/eit/it*

coun.ter.feit *adj.* made in imitation of something else with intent to deceive

Grammar Tips: -hypocrites *pl.*

Synonym: n/a

Sentence Completion: choose one rhyming word above to complete the sentence.

He is nothing but a_____, pretending that he knows nothing about it

Answer: *hypocrite*

hy.po.the.sis [haɪˈpɑθəsɪs] *n.* an assumption; a theory

rhyming memory sound –othesis

pro.the.sis *n.* the addition of a sound to the beginning of a word

Grammar Tips: -hypotheses *pl.*

Synonym: proposition

Sentence Completion: choose one rhyming word above to complete the sentence.

"We created our _____ through casual observation and examination of scholarly accounts," the authors said

Answer: *hypothesis*

I

i.co.no.clast [aɪˈkɑnəˌklæst] *n.* a rebel; one who breaks with tradition   *rhyming memory sound –ast*

en.co.mi.ast *n.* one that praises : eulogist

sym.po.si.ast *n.* a contributor to a symposium

Grammar Tips: -**iconoclasts** *pl.*,

-**iconoclastic** *adj.*, -**iconoclastically** *adv.*

                                                Synonym: bohemian

Sentence Completion: choose one rhyming word above to complete the sentence.

An _____ is someone who attacks established ideas and customs

                                                Answer: *iconoclast*

im.par.tial [ɪmˈpɑrʃ(ə)l] *adj.* without prejudice

rhyming sound –artial

par.tial *adj.* being or affecting only a part; not total

court-mar.tial *n.* a military court to try members of the armed services who are accused of serious breaches of martial law

Grammar Tips: -**impartially** *adv.*,- **impartiality** *n.*

                                                       Synonym: candid

Sentence Completion: choose one rhyming word above to complete the sentence.

She had an_____mind, and saw the two sides of a question clearly enough to find little to choose between them.

                                                     Answer: *impartial*

im.pe.rious [ɪmˈpɪriəs] *adj.* domineering; haughty

rhyming memory sound –erious

mys.te.rious *adj.* of, relating to, or constituting mystery

de.le.te.rious *adj.* of, relating to, or characteristic of delirium

Grammar Tips: -**imperiously** *adv.*,- **imperiousness** *n.*

Synonym: authoritarian

Sentence Completion: choose one rhyming word above to complete the sentence.

He was an instance of complete baseness of spirit, _____, cruel, and relentless when uppermost, abject and low-spirited when down.

Answer: *imperious*

im.per.tur.bable [ˌimpə(r)'tɜr(r)bəb(ə)l] *adj.* steady; calm

rhyming memory sound –able

im.pa.lpable *adj.* incapable of being felt by touch

im.per.me.able *adj.* not permitting passage (as of a fluid) through its substance

Grammar Tips: -**imperturbably** *adv.*,-**imperturbability** *n.*

Synonym: unflappable

Sentence Completion: choose one rhyming word above to complete the sentence.

Only by reading between the lines can one follow the unsparing analysis beneath the_____surface.

Answer: *imperturbable*

im.per.vious [ɪmˈpɜrviəs] *adj.* not capable of being affected

rhyming memory sound -ious

de.vious *adj.* moving without a fixed course

hi.la.rious *adj.* marked by or causing hilarity : extremely funny

Grammar Tips: -**Imperviously** *adv.*,- **Imperviousness** *n.*

Synonym: impenetrable

Sentence Completion: choose one rhyming word above to complete the sentence.

Mr Murray seems to be similarly_____to recent events in the Pearl River Delta.

Answer: *impervious*

in.cho.ate [ɪnˈkoʊət] *adj.* at an early stage   *rhyming memory sound –oate/oit*

in.tro.it *n.* a piece of music sung or played at the beginning of a worship service

Grammar Tips: -**Inchoately** *adv.*,-**Inchoateness** *n.*

Synonym: aborning

Sentence Completion: choose one rhyming word above to complete the sentence.

His belief that his mostly_____economic reforms would spur a new

level of production and productivity was a delusion.

Answer: *inchoate*

in.con.gruous [ɪnˈkɑŋgruəs] *adj.* unsuited: inappropriate

rhyming memory sound –uous

con.ti.guous *adj.* being in actual contact : touching along a boundary or at a point

e.xi.guous *adj.* excessively scanty

Grammar Tips: -**Incongruously** *adv.*,- **Incongruousness** *n.*

Synonym: amiss

Sentence Completion: choose one rhyming word above to complete the sentence.

He is taller than I had supposed. Wearing a black suit with a white shirt, his shock of white hair is_____against a cherubic face.

Answer: *incongruous*

in.ef.fable [ɪnˈefəb(ə)l] *adj.* not able to be described; unspeakable   ***rhyming memory sound –able***

com.mu.table *adj.* giving in exchange for another; exchangeable

in.du.bi.table *adj.* too evident to be doubted : unquestionable

Grammar Tips: -**ineffably** *adv.*,-**ineffableness** *n.*, -**ineffability** *n.*

Synonym: incommunicable

Sentence Completion: choose one rhyming word above to complete the sentence.

At the bottom of the steps she stands waiting, with a smile and_____joy, an attitude of matchless grace and dignity.

Answer: *ineffable*

in.e.xo.rable [ɪnˈeksərəb(ə)l] *adj.* unyielding

rhyming memory sound –orable

de.plo.rable *adj.* deserving censure or contempt

ig.no.rable *adj.* to refuse to take notice of

Grammar Tips: -**inexorably***adv.*,
-**inexorableness** *n.*,-**inexorability** *n.*

Synonym: relentless

Sentence Completion: choose one rhyming word above to complete the sentence.

But meanwhile, as you know, wonderful protagonists like Al Gore are noting the _____ rise in temperature, set in the context of that.

Answer: *inexorable*

in.ge.nuous [ɪnˈdʒenjuəs] *adj.* simple; innocent; naïve

rhyming memory sound –enuous

stre.nuous *adj.* marked by or uttered with forcefulness

te.nuous *adj.* weak and likely to change

Grammar Tips: -**ingenuity** *n.*

Synonym: genuine

Sentence Completion: choose one rhyming word above to complete the sentence.

Cyclical downturns are nothing new – the _____ and bold take advantage of such dips and seize their chance.

Answer: *ingenuous*

i.ni.mi.cal [ɪˈnɪmɪk(ə)l] *adj.* harmful; unfriendly

rhyming memory sound –ical

hys.te.ri.cal *adj.* feeling overwhelming fear or worry

sab.ba.ti.cal *n.* a period away from work when people such as college or university professors can study, rest, or travel

Grammar Tips: -inimicable *adj.*

Synonym: adversarial

Sentence Completion: choose one rhyming word above to complete the sentence.

The South had entangled itself in a severely conservative countermythology _____ to creative effort.

Answer: *inimical*

i.ni.quity [ɪˈnɪkwəti] *n.* wickedness   *rhyming memory sound –uity*

e.quity *n.* the practice of giving to others what is their due

i.ne.quity *n.* an instance of injustice or unfairness

Grammar Tips: *-iniquities pl.*

Synonym: corruption

Sentence Completion: choose one rhyming word above to complete the sentence.

Come, straggling lights into the windows of the ugly house and you who do_____therein, do it at least with this dread scene shut out.

Answer: *iniquity*

in.si.dious [ɪnˈsɪdiəs] *adj.* treacherous   *rhyming memory sound –idious*

in.vi.dious *adj.* tending to cause discontent, animosity, or envy

per.fi.dious *adj.* of, relating to, or characterized by perfidy

Grammar Tips: -insidiously *adv.*, -insidiousness *n.*

Synonym: treacherous

Sentence Completion: choose one rhyming word above to complete the sentence.

Few others would dare try to understand the motivations of such_____monsters.

Answer: *insidious*

in.ter.dict [ˈɪntərˌdɪkt] *v.* to prohibit; to ban   *rhyming memory sound –ict*

con.strict *v.* to stultify, stop, or cause to falter

re.tro.dict *v.* to utilize present information or ideas to infer (a past event or state of affairs)

Grammar Tips: -interdict *n.*

Synonym: ban

Sentence Completion: choose one rhyming word above to complete the sentence.

They have taken effective measures to_____the arising trend of coal mine accidents.

Answer: *interdict*

in.ter.po.late [ɪnˈtɜrpəˌleɪt] *n.* to insert between; to estimate *rhyming memory sound –ate*

ae.rate *v.* to supply or impregnate (as the soil or a liquid) with air

be.rate *v.* to scold or condemn vehemently and at length

Grammar Tips: -lated, -lating, -lates;

-interpolation *n.*, -interpolative *adj.*, -interpolator *n.*

Synonym: insinuate

Sentence Completion: choose one rhyming word above to complete the sentence.

A quaternion also represents the most efficient rotation

to_____between two orientations of an object.

Answer: *interpolate*

in.ter.reg.num [ˌɪntərˈrɛgnəm] *n.* a period a nation is without rule *rhyming memory sound –um*

scum *n.* a low, vile, or worthless person or group of people

slum *n.* a densely populated usually urban area marked by crowding, dirty run-down housing, poverty, and social disorganization

Grammar Tips: -**interregnums** *pl.*,-**interregna** *pl.*

Synonym: discontinuity

Sentence Completion: choose one rhyming word above to complete the sentence.

There is no_____between the death of one sovereign and the accession of the next.

Answer: *interregnum*

in.tran.si.gent [ɪnˈtrænsɪdʒənt] *adj.* stubborn; refusing to give in   *rhyming memory sound –ent*

fer.ment *v.* to be in a state of agitation or intense activity

por.tent *n.* something that foreshadows a coming event

Grammar Tips: -**intransigent** *n.*,-**intransigently** *adv.*

Synonym: adamant

Sentence Completion: choose one rhyming word above to complete the sentence.

If you decide that being right is what matters to you, you are too_____to be a boss at all.

Answer: *intransigent*

in.ve.te.rate [ɪnˈvetərət] *adj.*   firmly established: deep-rooted   **rhyming memory sound –erate**

mo.de.rate *adj.* avoiding extremes of behavior or expression : observing reasonable limits

con.fe.de.rate *adj.* united in a league : allied

Grammar Tips: -**inveterately** *adv.*

Synonym: bred-in-the-bone

Sentence Completion: choose one rhyming word above to complete the sentence.

Nominalists accordingly adopt the opinion that substance is a spurious idea due to our_____human trick of turning names into things.

Answer: *inveterate*

i.ro.ny [ˈaɪrəni] *n.* incongruity between expectations and actuality   **rhyming memory sound -ony**

har.mo.ny *n.* a situation in which people live and work well with other people, or in a way that does not damage things around them

sym.pho.ny *n* a long piece of classical music played by a symphony orchestra

Grammar Tips: -ironies *pl.*

Synonym: satire

Sentence Completion: choose one rhyming word above to complete the sentence.

She looked at me square in the eye, without a trace of _____ and stated, "I have no time for an intern."

Answer: *irony*

J

ju.ris.pru.dence [ˌdʒʊrɪsˈprud(ə)ns] *n.* science of law

rhyming memory sound –udence

pru.dence *n.* the ability to govern and discipline oneself by the use of reason

im.pru.dence *n.* the quality or state of being imprudent

Grammar Tips: -**jurisprudential** *adj.,* -**jurisprudentially** *adv.*

Synonym: n/a

Sentence Completion: choose one rhyming word above to complete the sentence.

It was on the basis of this_____that I gave my view at the Constitutional Affairs Panel meeting.

Answer: *jurisprudence*

jus.ti.fy [ˈdʒʌstɪˌfaɪ] *v.* to prove to be just; make precise

rhyming memory sound -ify

so.lem.ni.fy *v.* to make solemn

so.li.di.fy *v.* to make solid or more solid

Grammar Tips: -fied, -fying, -fies; justifier *n.*

Synonym: rationalize

Sentence Completion: choose one rhyming word above to complete the sentence.

Trying to _____ it that way is a bit like the efforts to put a dollar value on liberal-arts education

.**Answer:** *justify*

jux.ta.pose [ˈdʒʌkstəˌpoʊz] *v.* to place side by side

rhyming memory sound –ose

coun.ter.pose *v.* to place in opposition, contrast, or equilibrium

de.com.pose *v.* to separate into constituent parts or elements or into simpler compounds

Grammar Tips: -juxtaposition *n.*

Synonym: n/a

Sentence Completion: choose one rhyming word above to complete the sentence.

I am going to speak about corruption, but I would like to_____two different things.

Answer: *juxtapose*

K

kindle [ˈkɪnd(ə)l] *v.* to set on fire: to excite   *rhyming memory sound –indle*

dwindle *v.* to become steadily less : shrink

swindle *v.* to obtain money or property by fraud or deceit

Grammar Tips: -kindler *n.*

Synonym: illuminate

Sentence Completion: choose one rhyming word above to complete the sentence.

If Euclid failed to_____your youthful enthusiasm, then you were not

born to be a scientific thinker.

Answer: *kindle*

ki.ne.tic [kɪˈnetɪk] *adj.* pertaining to motion *rhyming memory sound –etic*

mi.me.tic *adj.* relating to, characterized by, or exhibiting mimicry

phre.ne.tic *adj.* frenzied; frantic

Grammar Tips: - **kinetically** *adv.*

Synonym: active

Sentence Completion: choose one rhyming word above to complete the sentence.

Over the next year in Afghanistan, there is likely to be a lot more killing – or "_____ activity" as Nato's top brass prefer to call it

Answer: *kinetic*

L

la.co.nic [ləˈkɑnɪk] *adj.* using few words; concise

rhyming memory sound –onic

bi.o.nic *adj.* having normal biological capability

eu.pho.nic *adj.* pleasing or sweet sound

Grammar Tips: -laconically *adv.*

Synonym: aphoristic

Sentence Completion: choose one rhyming word above to complete the sentence.

His _____ answers to my requests for directions were both unfriendly and abrupt.

Answer: *laconic*

lan.guid [ˈlæŋgwɪd] *adj.* sluggishing from weakness; spiritless

rhyming memory sound –uid

squid *n.* an instrument for detecting and measuring very weak magnetic fields

li.quid *adj.* flowing freely like water

Grammar Tips: -languidly *adv.*,**-languidness** *n,*

Synonym: listless

Sentence Completion: choose one rhyming word above to complete the sentence.

In the sunny haze of the_____hours, what vast vision of thine takes shape in the blue of the sky!

Answer: *languid*

lar.gess [lɑːˈdʒes] *n.* gifts that have been given generously

rhyming memory sound –ess

ab.scess *n.* a painful swollen area on your skin or inside your body that is infected and filled with pusunpleasant yellow liquid

e.gress *n.* a place or means of going out

Grammar Tips: variant: -largesse

Synonym: bestowal

Sentence Completion: choose one rhyming word above to complete the sentence.

In 2006, the donation had a value of $30 billion, making it the biggest philanthropic _____ in history.

Answer: *largess*

la.tent ['leɪt(ə)nt] *adj.* present, but hidden   *rhyming memory sound –atent*

pa.tent *adj.* not subject to misinterpretation or more than one interpretation

Grammar Tips: -latently *adv.*

Synonym: inert

Sentence Completion: choose one rhyming word above to complete the sentence.

I have always been regarded as someone mild in character. Never had I imagined that there was such a violent streak_____within me.

Answer: *latent*

le.ger.de.main [.ledʒərdə'meɪn] *n.* sleight of hand; deception

rhyming memory sound –ain

con.strain *v.* to force by imposed stricture, restriction, or limitation

re.frain *v.* to keep oneself from doing, feeling, or indulging in something and especially from following a passing impulse

Grammar Tips: French origin: **leger de main**

Synonym: conjuring

Sentence Completion: choose one rhyming word above to complete the sentence.

By a feat of_____, the magician produced a rabbit from his hat.

Answer: *legerdemain*

le.thar.gic [lə'θɑrdʒɪk] *adj.* dull; slow-moving; sluggish

rhyming memory sound –ic

bi.o.pic *n.* a movie based on the events of someone's life

he.re.tic *n.* a person who holds unorthodox opinions in any field (not merely religion)

Grammar Tips: -lethargically *adv.*

Synonym: dull

Sentence Completion: choose one rhyming word above to complete the sentence.

Her face looked so_____and pale, her body was very thin; she could barely open her eyes.

Answer: *lethargic*

li.cen.tious [laɪˈsenʃəs] *adj.* lawless; immoral; lewd

rhyming memory sound –entious

ab.sten.tious *adj.* the act or practice of abstaining

sen.ten.tious *adj.* given to or abounding in aphoristic expression

Grammar Tips: -licentiously *adv.*, -licentiousness *n.*

Synonym: concupiscent

Sentence Completion: choose one rhyming word above to complete the sentence.

To the _____ person, grace becomes a cheap gift that holds very little genuine value.

Answer: *licentious*

lim.pid [ˈlɪmpɪd] *adj.* clear, transparent   *rhyming memory sound –id*

tri.fid *adj.* describes a tail or organ that is deeply divided into three parts

py.ra.mid *n.* a large stone structure with a square base and walls with three sides that meet at a point on the top of the structure.

Grammar Tips: -limpidly *adv.,* -limpidity *n.*

Synonym: crystal

Sentence Completion: choose one rhyming word above to complete the sentence.

If it were merely a pain it would melt in _____ tears, reflecting its inmost secret without a word.

Answer: *limpid*

lo.qua.cious [loʊˈkweɪʃəs] *adj.* talkative   *rhyming memory sound –acious*

ca.pa.cious *adj.* containing or capable of containing a great deal

fu.ga.cious *adj.* lasting a short time : evanescent

Grammar Tips: -loquaciously *adv.*, -loquaciousness *n.*

Synonym: blabby

Sentence Completion: choose one rhyming word above to complete the sentence.

The Hairless Mexican ate with huge mouthfuls, enjoying himself vastly, his eyes shone and he was_____.

Answer: *loquacious*

lu.gu.brious [ləˈgubriəs] *adj.* sad; mournful   *rhyming memory sound –ious*

du.bious *adj.* giving rise to uncertainty

ru.bious *adj.* red; ruby

Grammar Tips: -lugubriously *adv.*, -lugubriousness *n.*

Synonym: cheerless

Sentence Completion: choose one rhyming word above to complete the sentence.

Henry James Senior encouraged his children to be serious but not _____, to be ambitious but unworldly.

Answer: *lugubrious*

M

mael.strom [ˈmeɪlstrəm] *n.* whirlpool   *rhyming*
memory sound –om

fan.dom *n.* all the fans (as of a sport)

ran.dom *n.* a haphazard course

Grammar Tips: -maelstroms *n.*

Synonym: vortex

Sentence Completion: choose one rhyming word above to complete the sentence.

Mr Dale believes that, caught up in this_____of fads, managers can overlook the obvious - hence the title of his book.

Answer: *maelstrom*

mag.na.ni.mous [mæg'nænɪməs] *adj.* generous

rhyming memory sound –animous

u.na.ni.mous *adj.* being of one mind : agreeing

pu.sil.la.ni.mous *adj.* lacking courage and resolution : marked by contemptible timidity

Grammar Tips: -**magnanimously** *adv.*, -**magnanimousness** *n.*

Synonym: lofty

Sentence Completion: choose one rhyming word above to complete the sentence.

Petitions are being got up to secure that slot; Mr Obama is being prevailed upon to be _____.

Answer: *magnanimous*

mag.ni.tude ['mægnə,tud] n. size; extent *rhyming memory sound –ude*

al.ti.tude. *n.* elevation especially above sea level or above the earth's surface

la.ti.tude *n.* an imaginary line around the Earth parallel to the equator

Grammar Tips: Latin origin: **magnitudo**

Synonym: significance

Sentence Completion: choose one rhyming word above to complete the sentence.

There is a question of _____ here that they seem to have missed.

Answer: *magnitude*

ma.laise [məˈleɪz] *n.* discomfort; uneasiness *rhyming memory sound –aise*

fraise *n.* an obstacle of pointed stakes driven into the ramparts of a fortification in a horizontal or inclined position

ap.praise *v.* to set a value on : estimate the amount of

Grammar Tips: French origin: **malaise**

Synonym: debility

Sentence Completion: choose one rhyming word above to complete the sentence.

The economy basically was kind of going nowhere and had inflation, which didn't seem to get cured – kind of a _____ in the economy.

Answer: *malaise*

ma.le.dic.tion [ˌmælə'dɪkʃən] *n.* curse   *rhyming memory sound –iction*

be.ne.dic.tion *n.* the invocation of a blessing

ju.ris.dic.tion *n.* the power, right, or authority to interpret and apply the law

Grammar Tips: -maledictions *n.*

Synonym: anathema

Sentence Completion: choose one rhyming word above to complete the sentence.

I heard the people's _____ against him.

Answer: *malediction*

ma.le.vo.lent [mə'levələnt] *adj.* ill will or hatred; dangerous, harmful   *rhyming memory sound –evolent*

be.ne.vo.lent *adj.* marked by or disposed to doing good

Grammar Tips: -malevolently.*adv.*

Synonym: vicious

Sentence Completion: choose one rhyming word above to complete the sentence.

Two more goblins, trying to edge past the shrieking couple into the room, were caught in the chain of_____magic.

Answer: *malevolent*

maud.lin ['mɔdlɪn] *adj.* excessively sentimental
rhyming memory sound –in

a.kin *adj.* related by blood : descended from a common ancestor or prototype

cha.grin *n.* disquietude or distress of mind caused by humiliation, disappointment, or failure

Grammar Tips: -maudlin *n.*

Synonym: cloying

Sentence Completion: choose one rhyming word above to complete the sentence.

He always becomes _____ after he's had a few drinks.

Answer: *maudlin*

maw.kish ['mɔkɪʃ] *adj.* sickeningly sweet; overly sentimental

rhyming memory sound –awkish

gaw.kish *adj.* gawky; awkward

haw.kish *adj.* relating to one who takes a militant attitude and advocates immediate vigorous action

Grammar Tips: -mawkishly *adv.*, -mawkishness *n.*

Synonym: maudlin

Sentence Completion: choose one rhyming word above to complete the sentence.

Although some nineteenth-century critics viewed Dickens's writing as _____, modern readers have found them profound and realistic.

Answer: *mawkish*

mer.cu.rial [mərˈkjʊriəl] *adj.* changeable; fickle; erratic *rhyming memory sound –urial*

seig.neu.rial *adj.* of, relating to, or befitting a seigneur

en.tre.pre.neu.rial *n.* one who organizes, manages, and assumes the risks of a business or enterprise

GrammarTips: -**mercurially** *adv.*, -**mercurialness** *n.*

-**mercurials** *pl.*, -**mercurial** *n*

Synonym: capricious

Sentence Completion: choose one rhyming word above to complete the sentence.

She has been a steady and successful finance minister, no mean feat with a boss as _____ as Nicolas Sarkozy.

Answer: *mercurial*

me.ta.phor [ˈmetəˌfɔr] *n.* figure of speech comparing two different things   *rhyming memory sound –or*

a.na.phor *n.* a word or phrase with an anaphoric function

war.ran.tor *n.* one that warrants or gives a warranty

Grammar Tips: -**metaphoric** *adj.*, -**metaphorical** *adj.*,

-**metaphorically** *adv.*

Synonym: conceit

Sentence Completion: choose one rhyming word above to complete the sentence.

Are the vampires just a _____ to suggest that girls are destined to be tempted by delinquents?

Answer: *metaphor*

mi.ti.gate ['mɪtɪˌɡeɪt] *v.* to make less severe, less mild

rhyming memory sound –ate

ad.vo.cate *v.* one that defends or maintains a cause or proposal

me.li.o.rate *v.* to ameliorate

Grammar Tips: -**mitigative** *adj.*, -**mitigatory** *adj.*, -**mitigation** *n.*, -**mitigator** *n.*

Synonym: allay

Sentence Completion: choose one rhyming word above to complete the sentence.

To be sure, the Obama administration is taking action to help the economy, but it's trying to _____ the slump, not end it.

Answer: *mitigate*

mo.di.cum ['mɑdɪkəm] *adj.* a small amount   *rhyming memory sound –um*

glum *adj.* broodingly morose

thrum *n.* a hair, fiber, or threadlike leaf on a plant

Grammar Tips: Latin orgin: **modicus**

Synonym: little

Sentence Completion: choose one rhyming word above to complete the sentence.

For the moment, however, injections of seawater appear to have created a _____ of stability inside the cores of the two reactors.

Answer: *modicum*

mor.dant ['mɔrd(ə)nt] *adj.* sarcastic; biting   *rhyming memory sound –ordant*

con.cor.dant *adj.* consonant; agreeing

dis.cor.dant *adj.* being at variance : disagreeing

Grammar Tips: -danted, -danting, -dants;

-mordantly *adv.*, -mordant *v.*, mordant *n.*

Synonym: acerbic

Sentence Completion: choose one rhyming word above to complete the sentence.

His political opponents feared his_____tongue, and even more his_____pen.

Answer: *mordant...mordant*

mul.ti..farious [ˌmʌltɪˈferiəs] *adj.* varied; having many parts *rhyming memory sound –arious*

gre.ga.rious *adj.* tending to associate with others of one's kind

ne.fa.rious *adj.* flagrantly wicked or impious : evil

Grammar Tips: -multifariousness *n.*

Synonym: divers

Sentence Completion: choose one rhyming word above to complete the sentence.

It is a sharp demonstration of the risks of exposing Hong Kong's market to the whims of China's _____ bureaucracy.

Answer: *multifarious*

my.riad ['mɪriəd] *adj.* infinitely vast in number   *rhyming memory sound –yriad/eriod*

pe.riod *n.* the completion of a cycle or a series of events

grace-pe.riod *n.* a period of time during which you are allowed to pay what you owe

Grammar Tips: -multifariousness *n.*

Synonym: divers

Sentence Completion: choose one rhyming word above to complete the sentence.

Australia is well-known for its_____deadly creatures, but the peanut-sized Irukandji remains rather mysterious.

Answer: *myriad*

N

na.dir [ˈneɪˌdɪr] *n.* lowest point   *rhyming memory sound*
-adir/ader

a.bra.der *n.* rubbing or wearing away by friction

e.va.der *n.* one who takes refuge in escape or avoidance

Grammar Tips: Arabic origin: **nadhir**.

Synonym: bedrock

Sentence Completion: choose one rhyming word above to complete the sentence.

At the_____of the recession Acme's sales had fallen 20% and it had laid off ten of its 125 employees.

Answer: *nadir*

nas.cent [ˈnæs(ə)nt] *adj.* coming into being; being born

rhyming memory sound –ascent/acent

ad.ja.cent *adj.* not distant : nearby

com.pla.cent *adj.* marked by self-satisfaction especially when accompanied by unawareness of actual dangers or deficiencies

Grammar Tips: Latin origin: **nascens**.

Synonym: inchoate

Sentence Completion: choose one rhyming word above to complete the sentence.

Just as there are signs of a_____US recovery, Washington may be about to douse whatever anaemic growth prospects are on offer.

Answer: *nascent*

ne.cro.man.cy [ˈnekrəˌmænsi] *n.* magic, especially that practiced by a witch   *rhyming memory sound –ancy*

geo.man.cy *n.* divination by means of figures or lines or geographic features

sy.co.phancy *n.* obsequious flattery; *also* : the character or behavior of a sycophant

Grammar Tips: -necromancer *n.*, -necromantic *adj.*, -necromantically *adv.*

Synonym: bewitchery

Sentence Completion: choose one rhyming word above to complete the sentence.

Fielding was not ashamed to practise a little_____.

Answer: *necromancy*

ne.fa.rious [nɪˈferiəs] *adj.* wicked

rhyming memory sound –arious

pre.ca.rious *adj.* depending on the will or pleasure of another

vi.ca.rious *adj.* serving instead of someone or something else

Grammar Tips: -nefariously *adv.*

Synonym: bewitchery

Sentence Completion: choose one rhyming word above to complete the sentence.

The Nile perch is_____yet applauded (in the short run). Don't be afraid to call it when you see it.

Answer: *nefarious*

neo.phyte [ˈniəˌfaɪt] *n.* a beginner; a novice   *rhyming memory sound –yte*

aco.lyte *n.* one who assists a member of the clergy in a liturgical service by performing minor duties

e.lec.tro.lyte *n.* a nonmetallic electric conductor in which current is carried by the movement of ions

Grammar Tips: Latin origin: **neophytus**

                                            Synonym: *convert*

Sentence Completion: choose one rhyming word above to complete the sentence.

Alarmingly, at least for a container-ship_____like myself, the world's biggest ship seems to have a crew of only 19.

                                              Answer: *neophyte*

ni.hi.lism [ˈnaɪəˌlɪzəm] *n.* total rejection of established laws

rhyming memory sound –ism

e.go.cen.trism *n.* concerned with the individual rather than society

se.cu.la.rism *n.* indifference to or rejection or exclusion of religion and religious considerations

Grammar Tips: -*nihilist n.* or *adj.*,-*nihilistic adj.*

Synonym: *n/a*

Sentence Completion: choose one rhyming word above to complete the sentence.

By contrast, the chilly Californian _____ of Robinson Jeffers was a refreshing tonic.

Answer: *nihilism*

no.men.cla.ture [ˈnoʊmənˌkleɪtʃər] *n.* a set of names or terms   *rhyming memory sound –ature*

ma.gis.tra.ture *n.* magistracy

le.gis.la.ture *n.* a body of persons having the power to legislate;

Grammar Tips: -*nomenclatural adj.*

Synonym: appellation

Sentence Completion: choose one rhyming word above to complete the sentence.

This group is examining five issues that include: _____; safety; radio-frequency emissions and efficiency; and standby measurement.

Answer: *nomenclature*

non.cha.lant [ˈnɑnʃəˌlɑnt] *adj.* unconcerned; casual

rhyming memory sound –ant

a.da.mant *n.* a stone (as a diamond) formerly believed to be of impenetrable hardness

co.ve.nant *n.* a written agreement or promise usually under seal between two or more parties especially for the performance of some action

Grammar Tips: -nonchalantly *adv.*

Synonym: complaisant

Sentence Completion: choose one rhyming word above to complete the sentence.

I am amazed that you can be so_____about the coming test when everyone else is so worried.

Answer: *nonchalant*

nos.tal.gia [nɑˈstældʒə] *n.* longing for things of the past

rhyming memory sound –algia

neu.ral.gia *n.* severe pain in a part of your body, caused by damaged nerves

Grammar Tips: -**nostalgic** *adj.*, -**nostalgically** *adv.*, -**nostalgist** *n.*

Synonym: homesickness

Sentence Completion: choose one rhyming word above to complete the sentence.

"As an old cold warrior, one of yesterday's _____ almost filled me with _____ for a less complex time," he said. "Almost."

Answer: *nostalgia*

nul.li.fy [ˈnʌləˌfaɪ] *v.* to make useless or ineffective

rhyming memory sound –ify

mor.ti.fy *v.* to subdue or deaden (as the body or bodily appetites) especially by abstinence or self-inflicted pain or discomfort

nul.li.fy *v.* to make null; *especially* : to make legally null and void

Grammar Tips: -lifies, -lifying, -lified

Synonym: abate

Sentence Completion: choose one rhyming word above to complete the sentence.

The most important of these endowed the courts with sweeping authority to review and _____ the ICC's rate decisions.

Answer: *nullify*

O

ob.du.rate [ˈɑbdərət] *adj.* stubborn; hard-hearted

rhyming memory sound –urate

in.du.rate *adj.* physically or morally hardened

bar.bi.tu.rate n. a salt or ester of barbituric acid

Grammar Tips: -obdurately *adj* ., -obdurateness *n.*

Synonym: affectless

Sentence Completion: choose one rhyming word above to complete the sentence.

Are you_____ in your convictions because of her ?

Answer: *obdurate*

ob.fus.cate [ˈɑbfəˌskeɪt] *v.* to confuse; to bewilder; to perplex   ***rhyming memory sound –ate***

ex.ter.mi.nate *v.* to get rid of completely usually by killing off

pro.li.fe.rate *v.* to grow by rapid production of new parts, cells, buds, or offspring

Grammar Tips: -cates, -cating, -cated;

-**obfuscation** *n,.* –**obfuscatory** *adj.*

                                              Synonym: becloud

Sentence Completion: choose one rhyming word above to complete the sentence.

This message might appear if you_____ the solution code.

                                              Answer: *obfuscate*

ob.no.xious [abˈnakʃəs] *adj.* objectionable; offensive

rhyming memory sound –ious

ca.pri.cious *adj.* governed or characterized by caprice

of.fi.cious *adj.* kind, obliging

Grammar Tips: -**obnoxiously** *adv.,* -**obnoxiousness** *n.*

Synonym: abhorrent

Sentence Completion: choose one rhyming word above to complete the sentence.

It seemed as if the lawyer was deliberately being as _____ as possible.

Answer: *obnoxious*

ob.se.quious [əb'sikwiəs] *adj.* excessively submissive; overly attentive   ***rhyming memory sound –ious***

fas.ti.dious *adj.* having high and often capricious standards : difficult to please

per.fi.dious *adj.* of, relating to, or characterized by perfidy

Grammar Tips: -obsequiouly *adv.,* -obsequiousness *n.*

Synonym: fawning

Sentence Completion: choose one rhyming word above to complete the sentence.

Those men are most apt to be _____ and conciliating abroad, who are under the discipline of shrews at home.

Answer: *obsequious*

ob.stre.pe.rous [ab'strepərəs] *adj.* boisterous; unruly

rhyming memory sound –ous

hor.ren.dous *adj.* horrible; dreadful

lu.di.crous *adj.* amusing or laughable through obvious absurdity, incongruity, exaggeration, or eccentricity

Grammar Tips: -obstreperously *adv.*, -obstreperousness *n.*

Synonym: blatant

Sentence Completion: choose one rhyming word above to complete the sentence.

Giles Gosling himself was somewhat scandalized at the _____ nature of their mirth.

Answer: *obstreperous*

ob.tuse [əb'tus] *adj.* slow to comprehend   *rhyming memory sound –use*

ab.struse *adj.* difficult to comprehend

pro.fuse *adj.* exhibiting great abundance : bountiful

Grammar Tips: -obtusely *adv.*, -obtuseness *n.*

Synonym: blunt

Sentence Completion: choose one rhyming word above to complete the sentence.

He also had little interest in the dispute so long as it was confined to _____ and theoretical bureaucratic backbiting.

Answer: *obtuse*

of.fense [əˈfens] *n.* an attack; a cause of displeasure

rhyming memory sound –ense

dis.pense *v.* to administer or bestow, as in small portions

in.cense *v.* to make furious

Grammar Tips: -offenseless *adj.*

Synonym: breach

Sentence Completion: choose one rhyming word above to complete the sentence.

A third_____would be charged as a misdemeanor punishable by a maximum $1,000 fine and a year's jail time.

Answer: *offense*

of.fi.cious [əˈfɪʃəs] *adj.* meddling: interfering   *rhyming memory sound –icious*

per.ni.cious *adj.* highly injurious or destructive : deadly

pro.pi.tious *adj.* favorably disposed : benevolent

Grammar Tips: *-officiously adv., -officiousness n.*

Synonym: interfering

Sentence Completion: choose one rhyming word above to complete the sentence.

As soon as she found I was really gone from Randalls, she closed with the offer of that_____Mrs. Elton.

Answer: *officious*

om.nis.cient [amˈnɪʃənt] *adj.* all-knowing   *rhyming memory sound –ient*

pro.fi.cient *adj.* well advanced in an art, occupation, or branch of knowledge

suf.fi.cient *adj.* enough to meet the needs of a situation or a proposed end

Grammar Tips: -**omnisciently** *adv.*

Synonym: *all-knowing*

Sentence Completion: choose one rhyming word above to complete the sentence.

Writing tests first also requires you to accept an uncomfortable fact about yourself: you re not perfect or_____.

Answer: *omniscient*

o.pu.lent [ˈɑpjələnt] *adj.* rich; luxurious   *rhyming memory sound –ent*

aug.ment *v.* to make greater, more numerous, larger, or more

dis.sent *v.* to withhold assent

Grammar Tips: -**opulently** *adv.*

Synonym: affluent

Sentence Completion: choose one rhyming word above to complete the sentence.

"You are sumptuous,_____, expensive," her father rejoined, "You look as if you had eighty thousand a year."

                                                       Answer: *opulent*

os.ten.sible [ɑˈstensəb(ə)l] *adj.* apparent; conspicuous

rhyming memory sound –ensible

ap.pre.hen.sible *adj.* capable of being apprehended

re.pre.hen.sible *adj.* worthy of or deserving reprehension : culpable

Grammar Tips: -ostensibly *adv.*

                                                       Synonym: assumed

Sentence Completion: choose one rhyming word above to complete the sentence.

Conversely, America's_____success in avoiding default in fact highlighted the growing dysfunction of its political institutions.

                                                   Answer: *ostensible*

P

pal.lid ['pælɪd] *adj.* pale; dull   *rhyming memory sound*
–allid/alid

va.lid *adj.* having legal efficacy or force

in.v.lid *adj.* being without foundation or force in fact, truth, or law

Grammar Tips: -pallidly *adv.*,-pallidness *n.*

Synonym: ashen

Sentence Completion: choose one rhyming word above to complete the sentence.

His hair had grown very gray in but a few weeks, his step slow, his face_____, his eyes sunken.

Answer: *pallid*

pa.na.cea [ˌpænəˈsiə] *n.* a cure-all; an answer for all problems   *rhyming memory sound –ea*

high sea *n.* the open part of a sea or ocean especially outside territorial waters

coun.ter.plea *n.* a replication to a legal plea

Grammar Tips: -panaceas *pl.*

Synonym: alixir

Sentence Completion: choose one rhyming word above to complete the sentence.

Eurobonds are the latest_____, recommended by many of the same people who assured us years ago that the euro would be a secure currency.

Answer: *panacea*

pa.ra.dox [ˈperəˌdɑks] *n.* a statement that seems contradictory, but probably true   *rhyming memory sound –ox*

pox *n.* a virus disease (as chicken pox) characterized by pustules or eruptions

de.tox *n.* detoxification from an intoxicating or addictive substance

Grammar Tips: -paradoxes *pl.*

Synonym: dichotomy

Sentence Completion: choose one rhyming word above to complete the sentence.

Blood-soaked pop theology for a doom-laden time, its effect that of a gripping yet reductive _____: it lifts us downward.

Answer: *paradox*

pa.ra.gon ['perə,gɑn] *n.* a model of excellence or perfection

rhyming memory sound –on

a.ma.zon *n.* a member of a race of female warriors of Greek mythology

bi.ath.lon *n.* a composite athletic contest consisting of cross-country skiing and rifle sharpshooting

Grammar Tips: -paragons *pl.*

Synonym: model

Sentence Completion: choose one rhyming word above to complete the sentence.

He is like one who, having watched a tree grow from its planting—a _____ of tenacity, insulation, and success.

Answer: *paragon*

pa.riah [pəˈraɪə] *n.* an outcast   ***rhyming memory sound –lah***

mes.siah *n.* a professed or accepted leader of some hope or cause

Grammar Tips: -pariahs *pl.*

Synonym: castaway

Sentence Completion: choose one rhyming word above to complete the sentence.

I suppose no one wants to be a social _____ at 21 – even for a big bag of cash.

Answer: *pariah*

pa.thos [ˈpeɪˌθɑs] *n.* pity; deep feeling   ***rhyming memory sound –os***

ba.thos *n.* the sudden appearance of the commonplace in otherwise elevated matter or style

e.thos *n.* the distinguishing character, sentiment, moral nature, or guiding beliefs of a person, group, or institution

Grammar Tips: Greek orgin: **pathein**

Synonym: poignancy

Sentence Completion: choose one rhyming word above to complete the sentence.

The_____of advice on saying no is particularly bad when you consider how hard the word is to say.

Answer: *paucity*

pau.ci.ty [ˈpɔsəti] *n.* scarcity; lack   *rhyming memory sound –ity*

fe.li.ci.ty *n.* the quality or state of being happy

fea.si.bi.li.ty *n.* capable of being done or carried out

Grammar Tips: Latin orgin: **paucitat**

Synonym: dearth

Sentence Completion: choose one rhyming word above to complete the sentence.

Edward sang the ditty with a simple, homely style-which was the same as saying with no style at all-and he made use of much_____.

Answer: *pathos*

pec.ca.dil.lo [ˌpekəˈdɪloʊ] *n.* a minor offense

rhyming memory sound –o

dy.na.mo *n.* a forceful energetic individual

em.bry.o *n.* a vertebrate at any stage of development prior to birth or hatching

Grammar Tips: -**peccadilloes** or **peccadillos** *pl.*

Synonym: n/a

Sentence Completion: choose one rhyming word above to complete the sentence.

A politician's sexual_____sometimes are fatal for his or her political career.

Answer: *peccadillos*

pe.jo.ra.tive [pɪˈdʒɔrətɪv] *adj.* having a negative effect insulting   *rhyming memory sound –orative*

ex.plo.ra.tive *adj.* exploratory

res.to.ra.tive *adj.* of or relating to restoration

Grammar Tips: -pejorative n.

Synonym: disapproving

Sentence Completion: choose one rhyming word above to complete the sentence.

Although the term "pyramid" may sound rather_____, it is true of all pension schemes.

Answer: *pejorative*

pellucid [pɪˈlusɪd] *adj.* transparent; clear   *rhyming memory sound –ucid*

lucid *adj.* clear to the understanding

Seleucid *n.* a member of a Greek dynasty ruling Syria and at various

times other Asia territories from 312 b.c. to 64 b.c.

Grammar Tips: -pellucidly *adj.*

Synonym: crystal

Sentence Completion: choose one rhyming word above to complete the sentence.

After reading these stodgy philosophers, I find his _____ style very enjoyable.

Answer: *pellucid*

pe.re.gri.nate ['perigri.neit] *v.* to travel from place to place

rhyming memory sound –ate

ad.vo.cate *v.* to plead in favor of

com.pli.cate *v.* to make complex or difficult

Grammar Tips: -peregrination *n.*

Synonym: walk

Sentence Completion: choose one rhyming word above to complete the sentence.

Jack has decided to _____ around Vancouver Island during the summer.

Answer: *peregrinate*

per.fi.dious [pərˈfɪdiəs] *adj.*   deceitful; treacherous; unfaithful   *rhyming memory sound –idious*

in.si.dious *adj.* awaiting a chance to entrap : treacherous

in.vi.dious *adj.* tending to cause discontent, animosity, or envy

Grammar Tips: -**perfidiously** *adv.*, -**perfidiousness** *n.*

Synonym: disloyal

Sentence Completion: choose one rhyming word above to complete the sentence.

There is no vice that doth so cover a man with shame as to be found false and_____.

Answer: *perfidious*

per.func.tory [pərˈfʌŋkt(ə)ri] *adj.* done without care; routine   *rhyming memory sound –ory*

self-glo.ry *n.* personal vanity : pride

vain.glo.ry *n.* excessive or ostentatious pride especially in one's achievements

Grammar Tips: -perfunctorily *adv.*, -perfunctoriness *n.*

Synonym: apathetic

Sentence Completion: choose one rhyming word above to complete the sentence.

The gathering ended with a_____ endorsement of the cartel's existing – and routinely flouted – production quotas.

Answer: *perfunctory*

per.ni.cious [pərˈnɪʃəs] *adj.* deadly; destructive

rhyming memory sound –icious

vi.cious *adj.* having the nature or quality of vice or immorality

a.va.ri.cious *adj.* greedy of gain : excessively acquisitive especially in seeking to hoard riches

Grammar Tips: -perniciously *adv.*, -perniciousness *n.*

Synonym: adverse

Sentence Completion: choose one rhyming word above to complete the sentence.

Do not use power to suppress opinions you think_____, for if you do, the opinions will suppress you.

Answer: *pernicious*

pers.pi.ca.ci.ty [.pəːspɪˈkæsiti] *n.* keenness of judgment

rhyming memory sound –acity

sa.ga.ci.ty *n.* the quality of being sagacious

te.na.ci.ty *n.* the quality or state of being tenacious

Grammar Tips: -perspicaciously *adv.*, -perspicaciousness *n.*

Synonym: keen

Sentence Completion: choose one rhyming word above to complete the sentence.

It was a marvelous effort of _____ to discover that I did not love her.

Answer: *perspicacity*

phlegm.ma.tic [flegˈmætɪk] *adj.* unemotional; cool; not easily excited   *rhyming memory sound –atic*

ecs.ta.tic *adj.* of, relating to, or marked by ecstasy

trau.ma.tic *adj.* relating to a disordered psychic or behavioral state resulting from severe mental or emotional stress or physical injury

Grammar Tips: - **phlegmatically** *adv.*

Synonym: affectless

Sentence Completion: choose one rhyming word above to complete the sentence.

Her_____response itself is now a driver in this financial crisis, and people will rightly blame her for any serious accident.

Answer: *phlegmatic*

pique [pik] *v.* to irritate or annoy   *rhyming memory sound* –*ique*

cri.tique *n.* an act of criticizing; *especially* : a critical estimate or discussion

ob.lique *adj.* neither perpendicular nor parallel : inclined

Grammar Tips: -piques, -piqued, piquing; pique *n..*

Synonym: aggravate

Sentence Completion: choose one rhyming word above to complete the sentence.

To_____his wife de Canted began to call Forestier "poor Charles".

Answer: *pique*

pithy ['pɪθi] *adj.* concise; to the point   *rhyming memory sound –ithy*

mythy *adj.* resembling, concerned with, or of a subject for myth

withy *n.* willow; *especially* **:** osier

Grammar Tips: -pithily *adv.*, **-pithiness** *n..*

Synonym: aphoristic

Sentence Completion: choose one rhyming word above to complete the sentence.

His_____comments knocked the bottom out of my argument.

Answer: *pithy*

plain.tive ['pleɪntɪv] *adj.* sorrowful; sad   *rhyming memory sound –ive*

re.live *v.* to live over again; *especially* **:** to experience again in the imagination

fu.gi.tive *adj.* running away or intending flight

Grammar Tips: -plaintively *adv.*, -plaintiveness *n.*.

Synonym: aching

Sentence Completion: choose one rhyming word above to complete the sentence.

The hostess stopped, with a fork in her hand, as Eliza's sweet but _____ voice arrested her.

Answer: *plaintive*

pla.ti.tude [ˈplætɪˌtud] *n.* a dull or trite remark

rhyming memory sound –atitude

la.ti.tude *n.* extent or distance from side to side

in.gra.ti.tude *n.* forgetfulness of or poor return for kindness received : ungratefulness

Grammar Tips: -platitudes *pl.*

Synonym: banality

Sentence Completion: choose one rhyming word above to complete the sentence.

It was a _____ to maintain the fiction that he was conferring a great boon on me.

Answer: *platitude*

ple.tho.ra [ˈpleθərə] *n.* abundance   *rhyming memory sound –a*

flo.ra *n.* all the plants that grow in a particular region

cy.clo.spo.ra *n.* any of a genus of sporozoans including one (*C. cayetanensis*) causing diarrhea in humans

Grammar Tips: -plethoric *adj.*

Synonym: abundance

Sentence Completion: choose one rhyming word above to complete the sentence.

The authorities on Nasdaq in particular have approved a _____ of reverse mergers with shell companies.

Answer: *plethora*

po.le.mic [pəˈlemɪk] *n.* a controversy or argument

rhyming memory sound –emic

en.de.mic *adj.* belonging or native to a particular people or country

pan.de.mic *adj.* occurring over a wide geographic area and affecting an exceptionally high proportion of the population

Grammar Tips: -polemicist *n.*

Synonym: disputant

Sentence Completion: choose one rhyming word above to complete the sentence.

But underlying his _____ lay a approval of manufacturers foisting goods on consumers that did not really need them.

Answer: *polemic*

pre.ca.rious [prɪˈkeriəs] *adj.* uncertain; dangerous; risky

rhyming memory sound –arious

hi.la.rious *adj.* marked by or causing hilarity : extremely funny

vi.ca.rious *adj.* serving instead of someone or something else

Grammar Tips: -precariously *adv.*, -precariousness *n.*

Synonym: gregarious

Sentence Completion: choose one rhyming word above to complete the sentence.

Almost a week later, Jennifer faced another consequence of her family's _____ financial condition.

Answer: *precarious*

pre.cis [preɪ'sɪ] *n.* brief summary   *rhyming memory sound –is*

de.bris *n.* the remains of something broken down or destroyed

vis-à-vis *prep.* face-to-face with

Grammar Tips: -précis *pl.*

Synonym: abstract

Sentence Completion: choose one rhyming word above to complete the sentence.

Every student has to give a _____ of the plot of the short story "Snake Girl" on Monday.

Answer: *précis*

pre.co.cious [prɪˈkoʊʃəs] *adj.* prematurely developed

rhyming memory sound –ocious

a.tro.cious *adj.* extremely wicked, brutal, or cruel : barbaric

fe.ro.cious *adj.* exhibiting or given to extreme fierceness and unrestrained violence and brutality

Grammar Tips: -precociously *adv.*, -precociousness *n.*, -precocity *n.*

Synonym: premature

Sentence Completion: choose one rhyming word above to complete the sentence.

A miserly duck, a vampire and pair of _____ kids are among the richest fictional characters, according to a ranking by Forbes.

Answer: *precocious*

pre.ten.tious [prɪˈtenʃəs] *adj.* showy; putting on airs

rhyming memory sound –entious

li.cen.tious *adj.* lacking legal or moral restraints; *especially* : disregarding sexual restraints

sen.ten.tious *adj.* given to or abounding in aphoristic expression

Grammar Tips: -pretentiously *adv.*, -pretentioussness *n.*

Synonym: affected

Sentence Completion: choose one rhyming word above to complete the sentence.

Putting MBA on your business card could be seen as _____ and a bit unprofessional.

Answer: *pretentious*

pri.me.val [praɪˈmɪv(ə)l] *adj.* of the earliest times or ages

rhyming memory sound -eval

shrie.val *adj.* of or relating to a sheriff

me.di.e.val *adj.* of, relating to, or characteristic of the Middle Ages

Grammar Tips: -primevally *adv.*

Synonym: ancient

Sentence Completion: choose one rhyming word above to complete the sentence.

To the great economist John Maynard Keynes, it was a "barbarous relic" of a _____ economic past.

Answer: *primeval*

pro.bi.ty ['proʊbəti] *n.* honesty; integrity   *rhyming memory sound –ity*

self-pi.ty *n.* pity for oneself; *especially* : a self-indulgent dwelling on one's own sorrows or misfortunes

edge ci.ty *n.* a suburb that has developed its own political, economic, and commercial base independent of the central city

Grammar Tips: Latin origin: **probitat**

Synonym: decency

Sentence Completion: choose one rhyming word above to complete the sentence.

A more enlightened Chinese currency policy is at least as important a component of that co-operation as greater _____ in US fiscal policy.

Answer: *probity*

pro.cli.vi.ty [proʊˈklɪvəti] *n.* inclination; tendency

rhyming memory sound –ivity

ac.cli.vi.ty *n.* an ascending slope (as of a hill)

af.fec.ti.vi.ty *n.* expression of emotions

Grammar Tips: -proclivities *pl.*

Synonym: affection

Sentence Completion: choose one rhyming word above to complete the sentence.

Yet America's practical outlook and openness to change foster respect for China's accomplishments as well as a _____ to solve problems.

Answer: *proclivity*

pro.mul.gate [ˈprɑməlˌgeɪt] *v.* to announce; to advocate

rhyming memory sound –ate

ab.di..cate *v.* to relinquish (as sovereign power) formally

a.cer.bate *v.* to irritate; to exasperate

Grammar Tips: -gated, -gating, -gates;

-promulgation *n.*, **-promulgator** *n.*

Synonym: advertise

Sentence Completion: choose one rhyming word above to complete the sentence.

After advice from its legal and regulatory affairs department, the company agreed to_____ a dress code.

Answer: *promulgate*

pro.pen.si.ty [prə'pensəti] *n.* inclination; tendency

rhyming memory sound −ensity

ex.ten.si.ty *n.* the quality of having extension

im.men.si.ty *n.* the quality or state of being immense

Grammar Tips: *-propense adj..*

Synonym: aptness

Sentence Completion: choose one rhyming word above to complete the sentence.

It would be too simplistic to put all of this down to a

cultural_____ to defer to bullying corporate bosses.

Answer: *propensity*

pro.pi.tious [prəˈpɪʃəs] *adj.* favorable *rhyming memory sound –itious*

se.di.tious *adj.* disposed to arouse or take part in or guilty of sedition

sur.rep.ti.tious *adj.* done, made, or acquired by stealth : clandestine

Grammar Tips: -**propitiously** *adv.*, -**propitiousness** *n.*

Synonym: auspicious

Sentence Completion: choose one rhyming word above to complete the sentence.

It had hardly been a_____beginning, but he had chosen his course, and would show no swerve.

Answer: *propitious*

pro.saic [proʊˈzeɪɪk] *adj.* dull; commonplace; unimaginative

rhyming memory sound –aic

ar.chaic *adj.* of, relating to, or characteristic of an earlier or more primitive time

for.mu.laic *adj.* of, relating to using a set form of words for use in a ceremony or ritual

Grammar Tips: -prosaically *adv.*

Synonym: average

Sentence Completion: choose one rhyming word above to complete the sentence.

The first and largest composition was in a decidedly_____location: a parking garage on the outer ring of the city.

Answer: *prosaic*

pro.scribe [proʊˈskraɪb] *v.* to denounce   *rhyming memory sound –ibe*

con.scribe *v.* to limit; to circumscribe

in.scribe *v.* to write, engrave, or print as a lasting record

Grammar Tips: -scribed, -scribing, scribes;

-proscriber *n.*

Synonym: ban

Sentence Completion: choose one rhyming word above to complete the sentence.

Federal regulations_____the use of electronic devices on board a plane while it is landing.

Answer: *proscribe*

pro.tean [ˈproutiən] *adj.* changeable; variable

rhyming memory sound –ean

cy.clo.pean *adj.* of, relating to, or characteristic of a Cyclops

e.pi.cu.rean *adj.* of, relating to, or suited to an epicure

Grammar Tips: Latin origin: **Proteus**

Synonym: adaptable

Sentence Completion: choose one rhyming word above to complete the sentence.

The eyes themselves were of that baffling_____gray which is never twice the same.

Answer: *protean*

pro.xy ['praksi] *n.* one who acts in place of another

rhyming memory sound –oxy

po.xy *adj.* relating to a virus disease (as chicken pox) characterized by pustules or eruptions

or.tho.do.xy *n.* the quality or state of being orthodox

Grammar Tips: -proxy *adj.*

Synonym: assignee

Sentence Completion: choose one rhyming word above to complete the sentence.

The Italian banks have troubles, but they seem to be acting as a _____ for the general health of Italy's sovereign debt.

Answer: *proxy*

pue.rile ['pjʊrəl] *adj.* childish; immature   *rhyming memory sound –ile*

de.cile *n.* any one of nine numbers that divide a frequency

distribution into 10 classes such that each contains the same number

of individuals

a.xile *adj.* relating to or situated in an axis

Grammar Tips: -puerilely *adv.*, -puerility *n.*

Synonym: adolescent

Sentence Completion: choose one rhyming word above to complete the sentence.

He was more interested in states of mind than in "_____ superstitions, Gothic castles, and chimeras."

Answer: *puerile*

pug.na.cious [pʌgˈneɪʃəs] *adj.* eager to fight; quarrelsome

rhyming memory sound –acious

ra.pa.cious *adj.* excessively grasping or covetous

sa.ga.cious *adj.* of keen and farsighted penetration and judgment

Grammar Tips: -pugnaciously *adv,*

-pugnaciousness *n,.* pugnacity *n.*

Synonym: aggressive

Sentence Completion: choose one rhyming word above to complete the sentence.

This view was a necessary consequence of his pessimistic estimate of human beings as selfish, uncooperative, and _____ creatures.

Answer: *pugnacious*

pul.chri.tude [ˈpʌlkrɪˌtud] *n.* beauty   *rhyming memory sound –ude*

for.ti.tude *n.* strength of mind that enables a person to encounter danger or bear pain or adversity with courage

mag.ni.tude *n.* great size or extent

Grammar Tips: -pulchritudinous *adj.*

Synonym: beauty

Sentence Completion: choose one rhyming word above to complete the sentence.

Nothing will do better than adorning by heart to get more _____ in vision. Apparel is a solitary art to change your mood.

Answer: *pulchritude*

punc.ti.lious [pʌŋkˈtɪliəs] *adj.* very exact; precise

rhyming memory sound –ilious

su.per.ci.lious *adj.* coolly and patronizingly haughty

Grammar Tips: -punctiliously *adv.*, -punctiliousness *n.*

Synonym: correct

Sentence Completion: choose one rhyming word above to complete the sentence.

The Japanese were particularly_____planners, typically looking ahead in great detail on a 10-year horizon.

Answer: *punctilious*

Q

quag.mire [ˈkwæɡˌmaɪr] *n.* a swamp; a difficult situation

rhyming memory sound –ire

be.mire *v.* to soil with mud or dirt

ac.quire *v.* to come into possession or control of often by unspecified means

Grammar Tips: -quagmires *pl.*

Synonym: dilemma

Sentence Completion: choose one rhyming word above to complete the sentence.

And deciding whether to turn down requests for Facebook "friends" is a social_____in itself.

Answer: *quagmire*

qui.es.cent [kwi'es(ə)nt] *adj.* at rest; motionless

rhyming memory sound −escent

can.des.cent *adj.* glowing or dazzling from or as if from great heat

fluo.res.cent *adj.* bright and glowing as a result of fluorescence

Grammar Tips: -quiescently *adv.*

Synonym: dull

Sentence Completion: choose one rhyming word above to complete the sentence.

Decades of repression have ensured that the opposition is_____in Egypt and virtually inaudible in Saudi Arabia.

Answer: *quiescent*

qui.xo.tic [kwɪk'satɪk] *adj.* extremely idealistic; not practical

rhyming memory soumd −otic

hyp.no.tic *adj.* of or relating to hypnosis or hypnotism

psy.cho.tic *adj.* of, relating to, marked by, or affected with psychosis

Grammar Tips: -quixotical *adj.*, -quixotically *adv.*

Synonym: idealistic

Sentence Completion: choose one rhyming word above to complete the sentence.

Mr Murdoch is clearly enthusiastic about his latest, _____newspaper war with The New York Times.

Answer: *quixotic*

R

ran.cor [ˈræŋkər] *n.* bitter resentment; hatred *rhyming memory sound –or*

an.chor *n.* a reliable or principal support : mainstay; an anchorman or anchorwoman

Grammar Tips: Latin origin: **rancere**

Synonym: animosity

Sentence Completion: choose one rhyming word above to complete the sentence.

I address you with neither_____nor bitterness, in the fading twilight of life, with but one purpose in mind: to serve my country.

Answer: *rancor*

re.buke [rɪˈbjuk] n. to scold; to blame   *rhyming memory sound –uke*

arch.duke *n.* a sovereign prince

blood fluke *n.* schistosome

Grammar Tips: -buked, -buking, -bukes; -rebuke *n.*

Synonym: admonish

Sentence Completion: choose one rhyming word above to complete the sentence.

In a country reputed for its orderliness, putting your shoes on a public seat often earns a quick _____ from passersby.

Answer: *rebuke*

re.cal.ci.trant [rɪˈkælsɪtrənt] *adj.* disobedient; hard to manage   *rhyming memory sound –ant*

im.plant *v.* to fix or set securely or deeply

com.plai.sant *adj.* marked by an inclination to please or oblige

Grammar Tips: -recalcitrant *n.*

Synonym: contrary

Sentence Completion: choose one rhyming word above to complete the sentence.

She greeted him now as though he were a _____ member of the family, rather than a menacing outsider.

Answer: *recalcitrant*

rec.ti.tude ['rektɪˌtud] *n.* honesty; moral uprightness

rhyming memory sound –ude

pre.lude *n.* an introductory performance, action, or event preceding and preparing for the principal or a more important matter

so.li.tude *n.* the quality or state of being alone or remote from society : seclusion

Grammar Tips: Latin origin: **rectitudo**

Synonym: decency

Sentence Completion: choose one rhyming word above to complete the sentence.

The progressive era still had a Victorian culture, with its _____ and restrictions.

Answer: *rectitude*

re.dun.dant [rɪˈdʌndənt] *adj.* repetitious; unnecessary

rhyming memory sound –undant

a.bun.dant *adj.* present in great quantity

Grammar Tips: -redundantly.*adj,*

Synonym: superfluous

Sentence Completion: choose one rhyming word above to complete the sentence.

This looks promising. The only thing left is to reduce the list once again by removing_____entries.

Answer: *redundant*

re.gur.gi.tate [rɪˈgɜrdʒɪˌteɪt] *v.* to rush or surge back (as undigested food) *rhyming memory sound –ate*

a.bo.mi.nate *v.* to hate or loathe intensely : abhor

re.cu.pe.rate *v.* to get back : regain

Grammar Tips: -tated, -tating, -tates

Synonym: n/a

Sentence Completion: choose one rhyming word above to complete the sentence.

For the exam, you must be able to _____ the information.

Answer: *regurgitate*

rep.lete [rɪ'plit] *adj.* well-filled   *rhyming memory sound –ete*

ob.so.lete *adj.* no longer in use or no longer useful

tri.ath.lete *n.* an athlete who competes in a triathlon

Grammar Tips: -repleteness *n.*

Synonym: blubbery

Sentence Completion: choose one rhyming word above to complete the sentence.

Everything in her person was round and _____, though without those accumulations which suggest heaviness.

Answer: *replete*

rep.ro.bate [ˈreproʊˌbeɪt] *n.* a wicked person

rhyming memory sound –ate

spe.cu.late *v.* to meditate on or ponder a subject

vi.brate *v.* to emit with or as if with a vibratory motion

Grammar Tips: -reprobatory *adj.*, -reprobative *adj.*, -reprobate *v.*

Synonym: villain

Sentence Completion: choose one rhyming word above to complete the sentence.

Frankness and kindness like Amelia's were likely to touch ever such a hardened little _____ as Becky.

Answer: *reprobate*

re.pu.di.ate [rɪˈpjudiˌeɪt] *v.* to reject; to disown

rhyming memory sound –ate

con.flate *v.* to bring together : fuse

con.ju.gate *adj.* joined together especially in pairs : coupled

Grammar Tips: -diated, -diating, -diates

Synonym: reject

Sentence Completion: choose one rhyming word above to complete the sentence.

Babbit utterly _____ the view that he had been trying to discover how approachable was Miss McGoun.

Answer: *repudiated*

res.cind [rɪ'sɪnd] *v.* to cancel; to repeal   *rhyming memory sound –ind*

exs.cind *v.* to cut off or out

pres.cind *v.* to withdraw one's attention

Grammar Tips: -rescinder *n.* **-rescindment** *n.*

Synonym: abandon

Sentence Completion: choose one rhyming word above to complete the sentence.

The actor shall not alter or_____his act except in accordance with the law or with the other party's consent.

Answer: *rescind*

ruse [rus, ruz]   *n.*   a skillful trick or deception   ***rhyming memory sound –use***

ab.struse *adj.* difficult to comprehend

re.cluse *adj.* marked by withdrawal from society

Grammar Tips: French origin: **reuser**

Synonym: subterfuge

Sentence Completion: choose one rhyming word above to complete the sentence.

Just as he finished congratulating himself on his innocent_____he was bumped hard by one of his opponents.

Answer: *ruse*

S

sa.cro.sanct [ˈsækroʊˌsæŋkt] *adj.* extremely holy

rhyming memory sound –anct/anked

tanked *adj.* drunk

spindle-shanked *adj.* spindle-legged

Grammar Tips: -sacrosanctity *n.*

Synonym: sacred

Sentence Completion: choose one rhyming word above to complete the sentence.

An open society does not treat prevailing arrangements as _____; it allows for alternatives when those arrangements fail.

Answer: *sacrosanct*

sa.ga.cious [sə'geɪʃəs] *adj.* wise   *rhyming memory sound –acious*

au.da.cious *adj.* intrepidly daring

lo.qua.cious *adj.* full of excessive talk

Grammar Tips: -sagaciously *adv.*, **-sagaciousness** *n.*

Synonym: wise

Sentence Completion: choose one rhyming word above to complete the sentence.

Wise, intelligent, whenever Saul was confused about what to do, he would always go to his _____ grandfather for advice.

Answer: *sagacious*

sa.lient ['seɪliənt] *adj.* significant; conspicuous

rhyming memory sound –ent

aug.ment *v.* to make greater, more numerous, larger, or more intense

seg.ment *n.* a portion cut off from a geometric figure by one or more points, lines, or planes

Grammar Tips: -saliently *adv.*

Synonym: conspicuous

Sentence Completion: choose one rhyming word above to complete the sentence.

In a period of austerity, suddenly the question of how society distributes its benefits and burdens becomes more_____.

Answer: *salient*

sanc.ti.mo.nious [ˌsæŋktəˈmoʊniəs] *adj.* hypocritical for religious belief   *rhyming memory sound –onious*

a.cri.mo.nious *adj.* caustic, biting, or rancorous especially in feeling, language, or manner

par.si.mo.nious *adj.* exhibiting or marked by parsimony

Grammar Tips: -sanctimoniously *adv.*, **-sanctimoniousness** *n.*

Synonym: holy

Sentence Completion: choose one rhyming word above to complete the sentence.

Some critics loved the film, while others did not, one calling it_____drivel. Some viewers were outraged by an interracial kiss.

Answer: *sanctimonious*

san.guine ['sæŋgwɪn] *adj.* cheerful; optimistic

rhyming memory sound –ine

bo.vine *adj.* of, relating to, or resembling bovines and especially the ox or cow

clan.des.tine *adj.* marked by, held in, or conducted with secrecy

Grammar Tips: -**sanguinely** *adv.*, -**sanguineness** *n.*, -**sanguinity** *n.*

Synonym: optimistic

Sentence Completion: choose one rhyming word above to complete the sentence.

The authorities were excessively_____about the existence of such a vast and undercapitalised organisation.

Answer: *sanguine*

scru.pu.lous ['skrupjələs] *adj.* honest; ethical; precise

rhyming memory sound –ous

rau.cous *adj.* disagreeably harsh or strident

fa.bu.lous *adj.* wonderful; marvelous

Grammar Tips: -**scrupulously** *adv.*, -**scrupulousness** *n.*

Synonym: ethical

Sentence Completion: choose one rhyming word above to complete the sentence.

Sir Leicester, for all his_____politeness, is unable to assist her, and is left behind.

Answer: *scrupulous*

scur.ri.lous [ˈskʌrələs] *adj.* coarsely abusive; vulgar

rhyming memory sound –ous

e.nor.mous *adj.* marked by extraordinarily great size, number, or degree

hu.mon.gous *adj.* extremely large

Grammar Tips: -**scurrilously** *adv.*, -**scurrilousness** *n.*

Synonym: abusive

Sentence Completion: choose one rhyming word above to complete the sentence.

She was frightened by an utterly false accusation and an utterly_____threat.

Answer: *scurrilous*

se.di.tion [sɪ'dɪʃ(ə)n] *n.* rebellion

rhyming memory sound –ition

ren.di.tion *n.* the act or result of rendering

a.bo.li.tion *n.* the act of abolishing

Grammar Tips: Latin origin: **seditio**

Synonym: rebellion

Sentence Completion: choose one rhyming word above to complete the sentence.

We are told that not just the_____Act can be used, so can the Internal Security Act which allows for detention without trial.

Answer: *Sedition*

sen.ten.tious [sen'tenʃəs] *adj.* concise; including proverbs

rhyming memory sound –entious

ab.sten.tious *adj.* the act or practice of abstaining

con.ten.tious *adj.* likely to cause disagreement or argument

Grammar Tips: *-sententiously adv., -sententiousness n.*

            Synonym: moralistic

Sentence Completion: choose one rhyming word above to complete the sentence.

Generally his ideas were expressed in brief _____ phrase, spoken in low voice.

            Answer: *sententious*

se.ren.di.pi.ty [ˌserən'dɪpəti] *n.* a talent for making discoveries by accident   *rhyming memory sound –ity*

pi.ty *n.* sympathetic sorrow for one suffering, distressed, or unhappy

me.ga.city *n.* megalopolis

Grammar Tips: *-serendipitous adj.*

            Synonym: providence

Sentence Completion: choose one rhyming word above to complete the sentence.

You think there's a sort of coincidence going on, a_____, in which you're getting all this help from the universe.

Answer: *serendipity*

ser.vile ['sɜrˌvaɪl] *adj.* like a slave   **rhyming memory sound –ile/il**

cher.vil *n.* an herb that is often used in cooking and salads

Grammar Tips: -**servilely** *adv.*,-**servileness** n., -**servility** *n.*

Synonym: base

Sentence Completion: choose one rhyming word above to complete the sentence.

On the first day shall be an holy convocation: ye shall do no_____work therein.

Answer: *servile*

so.journ ['souˌdʒɜrn] *n.* a brief stay or visit   **rhyming memory sound –urn**

213

ad.journ *v.* to suspend indefinitely or until a later stated time

ta.ci.turn *adj.* temperamentally disinclined to talk

Grammar Tips: -sojourn *v.*

                                                      Synonym: visit

Sentence Completion: choose one rhyming word above to complete the sentence.

And there was a famine in the land; and Abram went down to Egypt to_____there, for the famine was severe in the land.

                                                      Answer: *sojourn*

so.li.ci.tude [sə'lɪsɪˌtud] *n.* concern; anxiety

rhyming memory sound –ude

ap.ti.tude *n.* a natural ability

mag.ni.tude *n.* great size or extent

Grammar Tips: -solicitudes *pl.*

                                        Synonym: anxiousness

Sentence Completion: choose one rhyming word above to complete the sentence.

I would not on any account trifle with her affectionate_____, or allow her to hear it from anyone but myself.

Answer: *solicitude*

so.lip.sis.tic [ˌsɑlɪpˈsɪztɪk] *adj.* the theory of only oneself being existent   *rhyming memory sound –istic*

a.nar.chis.tic *adj.* relating to a person who rebels against any authority, established order, or ruling power

e.go.tis.tic *adj.* having an exaggerated sense of self-importance

Grammar Tips: -**solipsistically** *adv.*, -**solipsist** *n.*, -**solipsism** *n.*

Synonym: egocentric

Sentence Completion: choose one rhyming word above to complete the sentence.

The hypochondriac remains a disreputable figure, _____ and even immune to the real suffering of others.

Answer: *solipsistic*

som.no.lent [ˈsɑmnələnt] *adj.* drowsy; sleepy

rhyming memory sound –ent

la.ment *v.* to express sorrow, mourning, or regret for often demonstratively

re.pent *v.* to turn from sin and dedicate oneself to the amendment of one's life

Grammar Tips: *-somnolently adv.*

Synonym: drowsy

Sentence Completion: choose one rhyming word above to complete the sentence.

This debut of a major new radio program at the naval base had been stirring the_____territory for days.

Answer: *somnolent*

so.phi.stry [ˈsɑfɪstri] *n.* a deceptive, tricky argument

rhyming mempory sound –y

pas.try *n.* sweet baked goods made of dough having a high fat content

in.dus.try *n.* diligence in an employment or pursuit; *especially* : steady or habitual effort

Grammar Tips: -sophistries *pl.*

Synonym: sophism

Sentence Completion: choose one rhyming word above to complete the sentence.

They have been repelled by the apparent_____of parts of his essay on "Civil Disobedience".

Answer: *sophistry*

spe.cious ['spiʃəs] *adj.* not genuine; pleasing to the eye but deceptive   *rhyming memory sound –ious*

fu.ga.cious *adj.* lasting a short time

effi.ca.cious *adj.* having the power to produce a desired effect

Grammar Tips: -speciously *adv.,* -speciousness *n.*

Synonym: beguiling

Sentence Completion: choose one rhyming word above to complete the sentence.

This proprietary research is the antithesis of_____and self-serving published surveys.

Answer: *specious*

spu.rious [ˈspjʊriəs] *adj.* deceitful; counterfeit

rhyming memory sound –urious

pe.nu.rious *adj.* given to or marked by extreme stinting frugality

per.ju.rious *adj.* marked by perjury

Grammar Tips: -**spuriously** *adv.*, -**spuriousness** *n.*

Synonym: bogus

Sentence Completion: choose one rhyming word above to complete the sentence.

This is a banal untruth, uttered with an air of _____ profundity designed to embarrass people not on board for their project.

Answer: *spurious*

staid [steɪd] *adj.* sedate; settled *rhyming memory sound –aid*

raid *n.* a hostile or predatory incursion

Me.di.caid *n.* a program of medical aid designed for those unable to

afford regular medical service and financed by the state and federal governments

Grammar Tips: -**staidly** *adv.*, -**staidness** *n.*

Synonym: grave

Sentence Completion: choose one rhyming word above to complete the sentence.

I was surprised to see him at the jazz club; I always thought of him as a rather _____ old gentleman.

Answer: *staid*

stoic [ˈstoʊɪk] *adj.* showing no emotion; indifferent

rhyming memory sound –oic

a.zoic *adj.* having no living beings

a.ne.choic *adj.* free from echoes and reverberations

Grammar Tips: -**stoic** *n.*, -**stoics** *pl.*

Synonym: indifferent

Sentence Completion: choose one rhyming word above to complete the sentence.

Supremely, of course, the_____gets himself or herself into most difficulty when it comes to connivance and tolerance.

Answer: *stoic*

stul.ti.fy ['stʌltə,faɪ] v. make absurd or ridiculous; render worthless   *rhyming memory sound –ify*

nul,li,fy *v.* to make of no value or consequence

rec.ti.fy *v.* to set right

Grammar Tips: -stultification *n.*

Synonym: impair

Sentence Completion: choose one rhyming word above to complete the sentence.

The regular use of calculators could_____ a child's capacity to do basic mental operations.

Answer: *stultify*

stu.pe.fy [ˈstjupə,faɪ] v. to stun; to amaze   *rhyming memory sound –y*

amp.li.fy v. to make larger or greater

vi.li.fy v. to lower in estimation or importance

Grammar Tips: -fied, -fying, -fies; -stupefyingly *adv.*

Synonym: dumbfound

Sentence Completion: choose one rhyming word above to complete the sentence.

You've had another opportunity to try to _____ me.

Answer: *stupefy*

sur.feit [ˈsɜrfɪt] n. an excessive amount   *rhyming memory sound –eit*

con.ceit n. excessive appreciation of one's own worth or virtue

de.ceit n. the act or practice of deceiving

Grammar Tips: -surfeit v.

Synonym: plethora

Sentence Completion: choose one rhyming word above to complete the sentence.

The stimulus packages that have been announced across the region must try to turn its_____of savers into avid consumers.

Answer: *surfeit*

sur.mise [sə(r)'maɪz] *v.* to guess   *rhyming memory sound –ise*

ap.prise *v.* to give notice to

re.prise *v.* to recover by force

Grammar Tips: -surmise *n.*

Synonym: guess

Sentence Completion: choose one rhyming word above to complete the sentence.

You had no need to look at the red button that adorned his black coat to_____that he was a person of consequence.

Answer: *surmise*

sur.rep.ti.tious [ˌsʌrəp'tɪʃəs] *adj.* acting in a sneaky way *rhyming memory sound -itious*

pro.pi.tious *adj.* being a good omen

ad.ven.ti.tious *adj.* coming from another source and not inherent or innate

Grammar Tips: -surreptitiously *adv.*

Synonym: clandestine

Sentence Completion: choose one rhyming word above to complete the sentence.

She carried out a_____search of his belongings.

Answer: *surreptitious*

sur.ro.gate [ˈsʌrəgət] *adj.* substitute *rhyming memory sound –ate*

ger.mi.nate *v.* arranged in pairs

vin.di.cate *v.* to free from allegation or blame

Grammar Tips: -gated, -gating, -gates.

Synonym: substitute

Sentence Completion: choose one rhyming word above to complete the sentence.

And it has some out there ideas, like the guess that_____mothers might soon have salaries that match Wall Street.

Answer: *surrogate*

sy.co.phant ['sɪkəfənt] *n.* a flatterer; a parasite

rhyming memory sound –ant

con.fi.dant *n.* one to whom secrets are entrusted

non.cha.lant *adj.* having an air of easy unconcern or indifference

Grammar Tips: -sycophant *adj.*

Synonym: bootlicker

Sentence Completion: choose one rhyming word above to complete the sentence.

But I'll be damned if I'll be blocked by some_____in the white house.

Answer: *sycophant*

syn.the.sis [ˈsɪnθəsɪs] *n.* a combination; a fusion

rhyming memory sound –esis

the.sis *n.* a treatise advancing a new point of view resulting from research; usually a requirement for an advanced academic degree

ki.ne.sis *n,* a movement that is a response to a stimulus but is not oriented with respect to the source of stimulation

Grammar Tips: -syntheist *n.*

Synonym: amalgam

Sentence Completion: choose one rhyming word above to complete the sentence.

Literature must be an analysis of experience and a _____ of the findings into a unity.

Answer: *synthesis*

T

ta.ci.turn [ˈtæsɪˌtɜrn] *adj.* silent; not talkative

rhyming memory sound −urn

o.ver.turn *v.* to cause to turn over

slash-and-turn *adj.* extremely ruthless and unsparing

Grammar Tips: -taciturnity *n.*

Synonym: laconic

Sentence Completion: choose one rhyming word above to complete the sentence.

However, several times a day he telephones his wife and his_____manner is replaced by a sickly cooing.

Answer: *taciturn*

tan.gible [ˈtændʒəb(ə)l] *adj.* real; capable of being touched

rhyming memory sound −angible

fran.gible *adj.* capable of being broken

in.tan.gible *adj.* assets that are saleable though not material or physical

Grammar Tips: -tangiblity *n.*, -tangibleness *n.*

−tangibly *adv.*

Synonym: palpable

Sentence Completion: choose one rhyming word above to complete the sentence.

It was one of the first_____signs of the government's decision to raise fuel prices, which went into effect Tuesday at midnight.

Answer: *tangible*

tan.ta.mount [ˈtæntəˌmaʊnt] *adj.* equivalent to

rhyming memory sound −ount

re.count *v.* to relate in detail

pa.ra.mount *adj.* superior to all others

Grammar Tips: Anglo-French orgin: **tant amunter**

Synonym: equivalent

Sentence Completion: choose one rhyming word above to complete the sentence.

North Korea has held out the threat of more tests, calling U.S. Pressure to rein in its nuclear program_____to a "declaration of war.

Answer: *tantamount*

taunt [tɔnt] *v.* to ridicule; to insult **rhyming memory sound –aunt**

daunt *v.* to lessen the courage of

vaunt *v.* to make a vain display of one's own worth or attainments

Grammar Tips: -taunt *n.*

Synonym: insult

Sentence Completion: choose one rhyming word above to complete the sentence.

All day long my enemies _____ me; those who rail against me use my name as a curse.

Answer: *taunt*

te.me.ri.ty [tə'merəti] *n.* boldness; rashness   *rhyming memory sound –erity*

dex.te.ri.ty *n.* mental skill or quickness

pos.te.ri.ty *n.* all future generations

Grammar Tips: -temerities *pl.*

Synonym: audacity

Sentence Completion: choose one rhyming word above to complete the sentence.

Age looks with anger on the _____ of youth, and youth with contempt on the scrupulosity of age.

Answer: *temerity*

te.nuous ['tenjuəs] *adj.* slender; flimsy; without substance

rhyming memory sound –enuous

stre.nuous *adj.* marked by or calling for energy or stamina

in.ge.nuous *adj.* ingenious

Grammar Tips: -**tenuously** *adv.*, -**tenuousness** *n.*

Synonym: flimsy

Sentence Completion: choose one rhyming word above to complete the sentence.

Concentration of control of mass media has congealed at a _____ time in American history.

Answer: *tenuous*

tor.pid ['tɔrpɪd] *adj.* inactive; sluggish   *rhyming memory sound –id*

bi.fid *adj.* divided into two equal lobes or parts by a median cleft

re.sid *n.* residual oil

Grammar Tips: -**torpidity** *n.*

Synonym: inert

Sentence Completion: choose one rhyming word above to complete the sentence.

And under the influence of that wintry piece of fact, she would become _____ again.

Answer: *torpid*

trac.table [ˈtræktəb(ə)l] *adj.* easy to manage   *rhyming memory sound –able*

hos.pi.table *adj.* given to generous and cordial reception of guests

re.mit.table *adj.* sending (money) to a person in payment of a demand, account, or draft

Grammar Tips: -tractably *adv.*, -tractability *n.*, -tractableness *n.*

Synonym: amenable

Sentence Completion: choose one rhyming word above to complete the sentence.

The Nixon Administration deliberately withhold supplies from Israel to make it more _____ in negotiations.

Answer: *tractable*

tran.sient ['trænziənt] *adj.* temporary; passing

rhyming memory sound –ent

con.sent *v.* to give assent or approval

dis.sent *v.* to differ in opinion

Grammar Tips: -transiently *adv.*

Synonym: ephemeral

Sentence Completion: choose one rhyming word above to complete the sentence.

Add to this the fact that no one wants to be Billy No Mates and you have the recipe for an explosion of _____ and threadbare friendship.

Answer: *transient*

trans.mute [trænz'mjut] *v.* to change from one form to another   *rhyming memory sound –ute*

at.tri.bute *n.* an inherent characteristic

con.vo.lute *v.* to twist; to coil

Grammar Tips: -muted, muting, -mutes;

-transmutable *adj.*

Synonym: alchemize

Sentence Completion: choose one rhyming word above to complete the sentence.

Medieval alchemists attempted to_____base metals into gold.

Answer: *transmute*

tren.chant ['trentʃənt] *adj.* keen; vigorous; effective

rhyming memory sound –ant

pen.chant *n.* a strong and continued inclination

Grammar Tips: -trenchantly *adj.*

Synonym: keen

Sentence Completion: choose one rhyming word above to complete the sentence.

Many of her_____articles together with those of Rewi Alley can be found today in the old volumes of the magazine.

Answer: *trenchant*

tru.cu.lent [ˈtrʌkjələnt] *adj.* savage; brutal; cruel

rhyming memory sound –ent

re.pent *v.* content to turn from sin and dedicate oneself to the amendment of one's life

tor.ment *v.* the infliction of torture

Grammar Tips: -truculently *adv.*

Synonym: aggressive

Sentence Completion: choose one rhyming word above to complete the sentence.

I remember her bringing me up to a_____and red-faced old gentleman covered all over with orders and ribbons.

Answer: *truculent*

tur.gid [ˈtɜrdʒɪd] *adj.* swollen   *rhyming memory sound –id*

fri.gid *adj.* intensely cold

ri.gid *adj.* deficient in or devoid of flexibility

Grammar Tips: -turgidly *adv.*, -turgidity *n.*, -turgidness *n.*

Synonym: swollen

Sentence Completion: choose one rhyming word above to complete the sentence.

In more_____prose, but closer to the truth, was the father of modern capitalism, Adam Smith, and he said this.

Answer: *turgid*

tur.pi.tude [ˈtɜrpɪˌtud] *n..* baseness; shameful behavior

rhyming memory sound –ude

la.ti.tude *n.* extent or distance from side to side

al.ti.tude *n.* the vertical elevation of an object above a surface

Grammar Tips: Latin origin: **turpitudo**

Synonym: abjection

Sentence Completion: choose one rhyming word above to complete the sentence.

He has not been convicted of a crime involving moral_____.

Answer: *turpitude*

U

u.bi.qui.tous [juˈbɪkwɪtəs] *adj.* present everywhere

rhyming memory sound –ous

gra.tui.tous *adj.* given unearned or without recompense

i.ni.qui.tous *adj.* characterized by iniquity

Grammar Tips: -ubiquitously *adv.*, -ubiquitousness *n.*

Synonym: commonplace

Sentence Completion: choose one rhyming word above to complete the sentence.

Call centres have become_____as a tool for companies to sell their goods, gather information or deal with customers' complaints.

Answer: *ubiquitous*

umb.rage [ˈʌmbrɪdʒ] n. a feeling of resentment

rhyming memory sound –age

as.suage v. to lessen the intensity of

en.rage v. to fill with rage

Grammar Tips: Latin origin: **umbraticum**

Synonym: offense

Sentence Completion: choose one rhyming word above to complete the sentence.

Mary took_____over the fact that he changed what she had written for the newspaper without asking her.

Answer: *umbrage*

un.can.ny [ʌnˈkæni] adj. weird; strange   *rhyming memory sound –anny*

can.ny adj. clever; shrewd

cran.ny n. an obscure nook or corner

Grammar Tips: -**uncannily** *adv.*, -**uncanniness** *n.*

Synonym: arcane

Sentence Completion: choose one rhyming word above to complete the sentence.

The boy watched him with big blue eyes that had an _____ cold fire in them, and he said never a word.

Answer: *uncanny*

unc.tuous [ˈʌŋktʃʊəs] *adj.* oily; excessively polite

rhyming memory sound –uous

con.temp.tuous *adj.* manifesting, feeling, or expressing deep hatred

or disapproval

un.am.bi.guous *adj.* not ambiguous : clear; precise

Grammar Tips: -unctuously *adv.*, -unctuousness *n.*

Synonym: backhanded

Sentence Completion: choose one rhyming word above to complete the sentence.

If Mrs. Thatcher took any notice of all this _____ advice then there is no evidence of it.

Answer: *unctuous*

un.du.late [ˈʌndʒəˌleɪt] v. to move or sway in wavelike motion   *rhyming memory sound –ate*

be.rate v. to scold or condemn vehemently and at length

cas.trate v. to render impotent or deprive of vitality; to deprive of the testes

Grammar Tips: -undulate *adj.*

Synonym: ripple

Sentence Completion: choose one rhyming word above to complete the sentence.

Light purple waves_____in the center of the fan like a wall. The space behind it appears vast and open.

Answer: *undulate*

u.nique [juˈnik] *adj.* being the only one of its kind   *rhyming memory sound –ique*

an.tique n. any piece of furniture or decorative object or the like produced in a former period and valuable because of its beauty or rarity

bou.tique n. a shop that sells women's clothes and jewelry

Grammar Tips: -uniquely *adv.*, -uniqueness *n.*

Synonym: singular

Sentence Completion: choose one rhyming word above to complete the sentence.

Omega said the clock, with its _____ design for 2012, had been developed by experts and fully tested ahead of its launch.

Answer: *unique*

up.braid [ʌpˈbreɪd] *v.* to scold; to find fault with

rhyming memory sound –aid

gain.said *v.* to declare to be untrue or invalid

cham.ber.maid *n.* a maid who makes beds and does cleaning in a house or a hotel

Grammar Tips: -upbraider *n.*

Synonym: chastise

Sentence Completion: choose one rhyming word above to complete the sentence.

Do not_____an elderly man, but exhort him as a father, younger men as brothers.

Answer: *upbraid*

ur.bane [ɜrˈbeɪn] *adj.* refined; suave; citified   ***rhyming memory sound –ane***

bane n. poison; a source of harm or ruin

ar.cane *adj.* known or knowable only to the initiate: secret

Grammar Tips: -urbanely *n.*

Synonym: debonair

Sentence Completion: choose one rhyming word above to complete the sentence.

The enormous ballrooms, the cool café terraces beneath seductively_____Mitteleuropa arcades, the 1.3km of private beach.

Answer: *urbane*

u.surp [juˈzɜrp] v. to seize illegally   ***rhyming memory sound –urp***

burp *n.* the act or an instance of belching

slurp *v.* to make a sucking noise while eating or drinking

Grammar Tips: -usurpation *n.*, -usurper *n.*

Synonym: arrogate

Sentence Completion: choose one rhyming word above to complete the sentence.

In a flash the evil intent of the vice-president to_____power hit the president between the eyes.

Answer: *usurp*

V

va.cil.late [ˈvæsɪˌleɪt] *v.* to sway back and forth; to hesitate

rhyming memory sound –ate

a.dum.brate *v.* to foreshadow vaguely

ag.gre.gate *v.* formed by the collection of units or particles into a body, mass, or amount

Grammar Tips:. -**vacillatingly** *adv.*, -**vacillater** *n.*

Synonym: balance

Sentence Completion: choose one rhyming word above to complete the sentence.

Such parents_____between saying no and giving in -but neither response seems satisfactory to their children.

Answer: *vacillate*

va.lid ['vælɪd] *adj.* true; logical; sound   *rhyming memory sound –alid*

in.va.lid *adj.* having no cogency or legal force

Grammar Tips: -**validly** *adv.*, -**validity** *n.*

Synonym: coherent

Sentence Completion: choose one rhyming word above to complete the sentence.

You know that, with bankers, nothing but a written document will be _____.

Answer: *valid*

vapid ['væpɪd] *adj.* uninteresting; tasteless; tedious

rhyming memory sound –apid

rapid *adj.* marked by a fast rate of motion, activity, succession, or occurrence

sapid *adj.* having flavor

Grammar Tips: -vapidly *adv.*, -vapidness *n.*

Synonym: dull

Sentence Completion: choose one rhyming word above to complete the sentence.

Many economists, journalists, and politicians will have you believe that consumer culture will lead to a_____, empty life.

Answer: *vapid*

va.rie.gated ['veriə,geɪtəd] *adj.* having different colors; diversified *rhyming memory sound –ated*

cor.ru.gated *adj.* having corrugations

af.fi.li.ated *adj.* closely associated with another

Grammar Tips: -variegated leaf

Synonym: chromatic

Sentence Completion: choose one rhyming word above to complete the sentence.

However, what we do have now is a much more_____media ecosystem in which to kind of create this kind of value.

Answer: *variegated*

ve.ne.rate ['venə,reɪt] v. to regard with respect

rhyming memory sound –ate

a.cer.bate v. to irritate; to exasperate

de.ni.grate v. to attack the reputation of; to belittle

Grammar Tips: -rated, -rating, rates; -venerator n.

Synonym: adore

Sentence Completion: choose one rhyming word above to complete the sentence.

In Europe these days, it is relatively rare even to see anyone in military uniform, far less to _____ them in symbolic terms.

Answer: *venerate*

ve.ra.cious [və'reʃəs] adj. truthful; honest   *rhyming memory sound –acious*

e.da.cious adj. of or relating to eating

fu.ga.cious adj. lasting a short time

Grammar Tips: -**veraciously** *n.*, -**veraciousness** *n.*

Synonym: honest

Sentence Completion: choose one rhyming word above to complete the sentence.

Mr. Yates might consider it only as a _____ interruption for the evening, and Mr. Rushworth might imagine it a blessing.

Answer: *veracious*

ver.dant [ˈvɜrd(ə)nt] *adj.* green; flourishing   *rhyming memory sound –ant*

con.fi.dant *n.* one to whom secrets are entrusted

comp.lai.sant *adj.* marked by an inclination to please or oblige

Grammar Tips: -**verdancy** *n.*, -**verdantly** *adv.*

Synonym: green

Sentence Completion: choose one rhyming word above to complete the sentence.

Well, with some heavy February downpours following one of the driest Januarys on record, positively_____is the answer right now.

Answer: *verdant*

ve.ri.si.mi.li.tude [ˌverɪsɪˈmɪlɪˌtud] *n.* the appearance of truth   *rhyming memory sound –ude*

so.li.ci.tude *n.* the state of being concerned and anxious

vi.cis.si.tude *n.* the quality or state of being changeable

Grammar Tips: -verisimilitudinous *adj.*

Synonym: literalism

Sentence Completion: choose one rhyming word above to complete the sentence.

Her paintings are famous for their_____.

Answer: *verisimilitude*

vex [veks] *v.* to irritate; to annoy   *rhyming memory sound –ex*

a.pex *n.* the upper most point

vor.tex *n.* something that resembles a whirlpool

Grammar Tips: Latin origin: **vexare**

Synonym: aggravate

Sentence Completion: choose one rhyming word above to complete the sentence.

Shall they not rise up suddenly that shall bite thee, and awake that shall _____ thee, and thou shalt be for booties unto them?

Answer: *vex*

vi.ca.rious [vɪˈkeriəs] *adj.* taking the place of ; substituted

rhyming memory sound –arious

gre.ga.rious *adj.* tending to associate with others of one's kind

ne.fa.rious *adj.* flagrantly wicked or impious

Grammar Tips: -**vicariously** *adv.*, -**vicariousness** *n.*

Synonym: substitutionary

Sentence Completion: choose one rhyming word above to complete the sentence.

During the Renaissance with growing capitalism and freedom, the doctrine changed so there was no "*vicarious* liability."

Answer: *vicarious*

vi.cis.si.tude [vəˈsɪsə,tjud] *n.* unpredictable changes; ups and downs *rhyming memory sound -ude*

al.ti.tude *n.* the angular elevation of a celestial object above the horizon

for.ti.tude *n.* strength of mind that enables a person to encounter danger or bear pain

Grammar Tips: Latin origin: **vicissitude**

Synonym: mutability

Sentence Completion: choose one rhyming word above to complete the sentence.

Social experience e.g Post-modernism is the phenomenon of this social experience and is the process and result of cultural_____.

Answer: *vicissitude*

vi.li.fy ['vɪlɪˌfaɪ] v. to speak evil of; to defame   *rhyming memory sound –ify*

pe.tri.fy v. to make rigid or inert like stone

rec.ti.fy v. to set right; to correct by removing errors

GrammarTips: -vilifier n.

Synonym: asperse

Sentence Completion: choose one rhyming word above to complete the sentence.

The politicians in Washington can get more votes by holding televised hearings where they _____ the oil companies.

Answer: *vilify*

viscous ['vɪskəs] adj. sticky   *rhyming sound –ous*

horrendous *adj.* horrible; dreadful

ludicrous *adj.* amusing or laughable through obvious absurdity, incongruity, exaggeration, or eccentricity

Grammar Tips: -viscously *adv.*, -viscousness *n.*

Synonym: ropy

Sentence Completion: choose one rhyming word above to complete the sentence.

Black oil is washing ashore, at least one person drowned in the_____oil slick, and efforts to clean up the mess are floundering.

Answer: *viscous*

vi.tri.o.lic [ˌvɪtriˈalɪk] *adj.* biting; sharp; bitter

rhyming memory sound –olic

hy.per.bo.lic *adj.* of, relating to, or marked by hyperbole

me.lan.cho.lic *adj.* of, relating to, or subject to melancholy

Grammar Tips: -vitriol *n.*

Synonym: bitter

Sentence Completion: choose one rhyming word above to complete the sentence.

He launched a_____attack on the prime minister, accusing him of shielding corrupt friends.

Answer: *vitriolic*

vi.tu.pe.rate [vaɪˈtjupə,ret] *v.* to scold; to criticize

rhyming memory sound –ate

ac.ce.le.rate *v.* to cause to move faster

ad.ju.di.cate *v.* to settle judicially

Grammar Tips: -rated, -rating, -rates

Synonym: scold

Sentence Completion: choose one rhyming word above to complete the sentence.

The preacher ascended the pulpit and _____ the parishioners for a litany of vices.

Answer: *vituperated*

vo.ra.cious [vəˈreɪʃəs] *adj.* extremely hungry; greedy

rhyming memory sound –acious

te.na.cious *adj.* persistent in maintaining, adhering to, or seeking something valued or desired

ve.ra.cious *adj.* truthful; honest

Grammar Tips: -voraciously *adv.*, -voraciousness *n.*

Synonym: edacious

Sentence Completion: choose one rhyming word above to complete the sentence.

The_____lady was gazing at the diamond necklace in such a way as a hungry boy was longing for the bread at the bakery.

Answer: *voracious*

W

wan.ton [ˈwɑntən] *adj.* reckless; immoral   *rhyming memory sound –on*

dea.con *n.* a subordinate officer in a Christian church

trea.son *n.* the betrayal of a trust : treachery

Grammar Tips: -wantonly *adv.*, -wantonness *n.*

Synonym: bawdy

Sentence Completion: choose one rhyming word above to complete the sentence.

She had rather suspected some of those_____trollops, who gave themselves airs because, forsooth, they thought themselves handsome.

Answer: *wanton*

wa.ry ['weri] *adj.* cautious; watchful   ***rhyming memory sound –ary***

con.tra.ry *adj.* a fact or condition incompatible with another

va.ga.ry *adj.* an erratic, unpredictable, or extravagant manifestation, action, or notion

Grammar Tips: -**warily** *adv.,* -**wariness** *n.*

Synonym: alert

Sentence Completion: choose one rhyming word above to complete the sentence.

Random recipient Michelle Kitson was confused and_____at first but decided to reply and the two began exchanging messages.

Answer: *wary*

win.some ['wɪnsəm] *adj.* pleasing; charming

rhyming memory sound –ome

awe.some *adj.* expressive of awe

trouble.some *adj.* diffcult; burdensome

Grammar Tips: -**winsomely** *adv.,* -**winsomeness** *n.*

Synonym: blithe

Sentence Completion: choose one rhyming word above to complete the sentence.

Just then she opened her eyes and gave him a _____ smile.

Answer: *winsome*

wry [raɪ] *adj.* produced by distorting the face **rhyming**
memory sound –y

a.wry *adv.* or *adj.* in a turned or twisted position or direction

de.cry *v.* to express strong disapproval of

Grammar Tips: -wry *v.*

Synonym: twist

Sentence Completion: choose one rhyming word above to complete the sentence.

When I asked if it would get any easier, he replied with a _____ smile: "Just a little."

Answer: *wry*

X

xe.no.pho.bia [ˌzenəˈfoʊbiə] *n.* fear of foreigners or strangers *rhyming memory sound –obia*

ae.ro.pho.bia *n.* fear or strong dislike of flying

claus.tro.pho.bia *n.* abnormal dread of being in closed or narrow spaces

Grammar Tips: New Latin: xenophobia

Synonym: n/a

Sentence Completion: choose one rhyming word above to complete the sentence.

Just as strikingly, the decline of empire has repeatedly coincided with intolerance and _____.

Answer: *xenophobia*

Y

yen [jen] v. an intense desire: a longing *rhyming memory sound –en*

fen *n.* low land

glen *n.* a secluded narrow valley

Grammar Tips: -yen *n.*

Synonym: yearn

Sentence Completion: choose one rhyming word above to complete the sentence.

Jennifer is always_____for something that does not exist in this world.

Answer: *yenning*

Z

ze.nith [ˈzenɪθ] *n.* the highest point   *rhyming memory sound –ith*

frith *n.* estuary

kith *n.* familiar friends, neighbors, or relatives

Grammar Tips: -zeniths *pl.*

Synonym: acme

Sentence Completion: choose one rhyming word above to complete the sentence.

She passed over the constellation of the Twins, and was now nearing the half-way point between the horizon and the_____.

Answer: *zenith*

ABOUT THE AUTHOR

Dr. Richard Lee is a professor of English and distinguished publishing scholar with more than ten books published under his name. His books are available on Amazon, other online stores, and in bookstores worldwide. Dr. Lee pursued his graduate education at the University of Rochester and the University of British Columbia and got his Ph.D. in English. He lives in beautiful Vancouver, British Columbia.

www.ingramcontent.com/pod-product-compliance
Lightning Source LLC
LaVergne TN
LVHW051043080426
835508LV00019B/1669